THE
WOMAN
EQUESTRIAN

Jane R. Slaughter

Wish Publishing
Terre Haute, Indiana
www.wishpublishing.com

LCCN: 2003101479

Proofread by Kim Heusel
Cover designed by Phil Velikan
Cover photo of Taylor Slaughter by Lee Photography
Interior artwork by Sandra Kabler (Chapter Four: Horses in Motion illustrations), Phil Velikan (Chapter Four: Saddles; Chapter Five: Anatomy of a Horse; Chapter Five: Hoof Diagram), Jane Slaughter (Chapter Four: Parts of Saddle),
Interior photos (except where noted in the text): from the collection at *www.arttoday.com*.

Every reasonable effort has been made to obtain reprint permissions. The publisher will gladly receive information that will help rectify any inadvertant errors or omissions in subsequent editions.

Printed in the United States of America
10 9 8 7 6 5 4 3 2 1

Published in the United States by
Wish Publishing
P.O. Box 10337
Terre Haute, Indiana 47801, USA
www.wishpublishing.com

Distributed in the United States by
Cardinal Publishers Group
7301 Georgetown Road, Suite 118
Indianapolis, Indiana 46268
www.cardinalpub.com

THIS BOOK

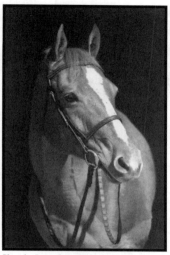

is dedicated to my horse, Sailor, clearly my definition of "Heaven on Earth." He stands tall, draped in chestnut, flashing a white blaze, that runs the length of his face. His warm, dark eyes and soft nicker are the welcome mat he offers with each meeting.

The sense of freedom I feel as Sailor and I traverse the landscape of a spring meadow has no equal. A fallen tree resting quietly before us offers an unexpected challenge to our ride.

Throughout the summer months, my soul mate and I participate in as many horse shows as we can squeeze into a handful of days. Sailor marches smartly around the ring during the flat class and snaps his knees to his chin over the jumps. Working as two individuals with one heart, we have never walked away emptyhanded.

The amber colors of fall offer a spectacular backdrop for our late-day trail rides. Meandering our way down a well-worn path, we are sheltered from the sun by a canopy of autumn hardwoods, as Sailor's hooves scatter the carpet of fallen leaves. The long shadows of the afternoon and the crisp air reenforce the notion that winter is just ahead.

In mid-December, I prepare Sailor for our annual Christmas caroling via horseback by wrapping a garland around his neck and tying a red bow at the bottom. He never complains about the adornments as my friends and I ride, singing in full chorus, from one farm to the next. With a light dusting of snow resting gently on the shady side of the hills, we find shelter in the indoor ring and long for the warmer days of spring.

Sailor is no longer a young man, but his spirit runs true and deep. Every ride is the safest trip he can muster and is offered freely without condition. The bond we have is quite incredible. A truer gentleman, I have never known!

Sailor, this book is for you.

PREFACE

I am not an equestrian of Olympic ability, nor am I a trainer of global status. I am, however, a woman who has loved horses and riding for a lifetime.

How then am I qualified to write *The Woman Equestrian*? Quite simply, I am a woman and I am an equestrian. I also possess a working knowledge of the sport and of the issues that are unique to women. Bouncing a small child on one hip and a basket of folded clothes on the other cannot be learned in a day; it requires practice, as does riding. The art of juggling a job, family, and friends while attending to your own needs, demands determination, as does riding. Careful attention to the balancing of your diet, your emotions, and your time requires intense focus, as does riding. Life is a "casserole," and it's only as good as the ingredients you choose to blend together. I am a mother, a student of riding, and a teacher of art. I am no different from you. I am a woman filled with a passion for my chosen sport and the dedication it requires. All of this, I believe, qualifies me to author this book.

It is my hope that reading *The Woman Equestrian* brings you mental clarity, emotional strength, and an unquenchable thirst for the ride!

Jane R. Slaughter

TABLE OF CONTENTS

Acknowledgments   ix
Foreword   xii
Introduction   xvii

Section One:
A History of the Woman Equestrian   1

Section Two: The Female Equestrian   21

Choosing an Instructor
What to Wear
The First Lessons
Choosing a Stable

Section Three: The Feminine Self   33

Voices: Mental and Emotional
Time Management
Proper Nutrition
Exercise: In and Out of the Saddle

Section Four: How to Ride   77

The Basic Concepts
Basic Equipment
Going to a Show
Horse Talk: A Glossary

Section Five: It's Not Just You 139

A History of the Horse
Diagrams of the Horse
Stable Care
Shoeing

Section Six: Disciplines 173

Dressage
Eventing
Hunting
Polo
Racing
Show Jumping
Steeplechasing

Afterword 208
About the Author 217

ACKNOWLEDGMENTS

When taking on the task of putting a book together, the list of people to thank and recognize becomes long, but necessary. The order in which names appear here is in no way proportionate to the order of significance of the individual's contribution. Each person's help, in his or her area of expertise, was of immeasurable importance in the writing of *The Woman Equestrian*.

THANKS.....

- To my daughters, Leigh Anne and Taylor; my mother, Cornelia L. Rankin; my brother and sister-in-law, Sam and Missy Rankin. Thanks for your support, your inspiration, and the push to keep me going. I'll love you forever.

- To my father, the late Sam A. Rankin Sr., a deeply missed friend, a lover of animals, a proud parent, and my guardian angel, thank you for watching over me.

- To Cathy Schlaeppi, my first trainer, thanks for helping me realize my dream of lessons and showing. Thanks also for giving me the push to write my first article for *The Chronicle of the Horse* magazine.

- To my trainer, Sandra Kabler, my instructor, technical editor, computer genius, artistic creator of the stippling illustration and the horses in motion, I thank you. She has the patience of a saint!

- To my "riding buddies," culinary geniuses, voices of encouragement, and shoulders to cry on, I offer a heartfelt thank you to Sally Thompson and Gillian Overing, the world's best friends.

- To Karen O'Connor, equestrian extraordinaire, and Olympic medalist, for writing the foreword for *The Woman Equestrian.*

- To Suzanne Lacy, an accomplished equestrian, a friend, a teacher, and an inspiration to all of her riding students (myself included), thanks for writing the afterword for this book.

- To all of the women and children who ride at the Sandy River Equestrian Center in Axton, Virginia.; Nicole Acuff, Alexis Aimee, Stephanie Bandyk, Grace Ann Edgerton, Sarah Margaret Dietz, Leah Hall, Katherine Sibbick, Franz-Hahr Phillips, Liz Goldstein, Susan Emmert, Vicki Meder-Williams, Nancy Ross, Robin Willis, Hilary Moore, Leisa Hall, and Nancy Moore, thanks for offering yourselves and your horses for purposes of pictorial illustration. I sincerely appreciate your time.

- To all of my fellow equestrians at the Triple L Ranch — Katie Zseltvay, Cory Meyer, Callie Fagg, Harriet Gayle, and Susan Weinbaum — for giving freely of their time for purposes of pictorial illustrations in the book.

- To Dr. Charese Pelham, thanks for training and placing on the market the world's best horse, my treasured Sailor.

- To Jason Cannon for his willingness to review my text and his helpful suggestions in the early stages of my book. I appreciated his enthusiasm.

- To Jean Kiger for graciously reviewing my entire text. I am grateful to her for giving freely of her time to read and — sometimes re-read — each chapter.

- To the owners of the Triple L Ranch, Ron and Barbara Lassiter, for their patience and understanding during my work on this book and the excellent care they provide daily for my horse, Sailor.

- To Dr. Richard Weinbaum for volunteering his time and talents for most of the candid snapshots found in the instructional sections, as well as the backcover color photo.

- To my yoga instructor Roxanne Gilgallon for her contribution regarding yoga and today's equestrian.

- To my yoga friends and classmates, Gayle Sink and Cathy Bencini, for giving freely of their time and talents for purposes of pictorial illustrations in the exercise section of the book.

- To John H. Burns, my teaching colleague and the digital photographer for the yoga pictures.

- To the entire faculty and staff of Thomasville Middle School for their support, help, and words of encouragement.

- To all of my art students at Thomasville Middle School in Thomasville, North Carolina, for offering their ears and opinions as I read aloud each chapter and verse of this book. I do appreciate their willingness to listen.

- To Robert K. Weber, Librarian/Archivist at The National Sporting Library in Middleburg, Virginia, for digging deeply in search of much-needed photographs and information.

- And lastly, to Holly Kondras, publisher of Wish Publishing, for believing in my ability to author this book.

FOREWORD

Women and horses have shared a common thread in the fabric of their lives for as long as humans and horses have interacted. However, it is only in the modern day, and not even throughout the world, that women and horses have reached the point in civilization, where society has decided it is now tolerable for them to reach their own potential, as individuals. Until the last 75 years or so, the horse has been used and often abused at the hands of man. He has been a beast of burden, a vehicle for hunting and travel, as well as a tool of warfare for literally thousands of years. It is true: the horse's contribution has been quite remarkable. But, that has come with a heavy price. The thought of losing one and a half million horses to our own Civil War in the United States, and most of them, to have died of disease and famine, is a daunting reality. Likewise, the woman, through history, has enjoyed little or no credit for her role. Other than that of the mother to a man's children, the woman had never been allowed to progress either physically or mentally until this past century. Women at the highest levels of power, either financially or politically, were normally born or wed into that role.

It is interesting to note that there are still many countries that favor the oppression of women. However, most of those countries either have no horses at all, or the horses are still to this day sentenced to a life of burden

Photo courtesy of Karen O'Connor

Karen at age 12 with her horse Shamrock; they were quite a team!

due to their own strength and stamina. As I have read this great book, *The Woman Equestrian*, the amazing, pioneering women who lived before us have fascinated me. I also started to realize that their courage made small and painfully incremental changes to the reality of equality. It wasn't until the male made changes in civilization, that the roles of both horses and women would change forever. I began to understand why, generally speaking, the relationship between women and horses can be quite different to that of the male and the horse.

With the invention of the combustible engine, all would change for man. Much of this change he had accounted for. While some of the effect of the change, no one could see coming. Now, machines would have the strength of a hundred men or more. People, men and women alike, would soon be judged by their intellect and the content of their character, rather than just by their raw strength alone.

Karen with "March Brown," receiving her 10th-place honors from the Queen of England. This was Karen's first international competition.

The engine would also change the horse's role in the world. There would no longer be a need for the horse for the survival of man. Nor is there a practicality to returning all the horses to the wild they once knew. The horse would now be used as a sporting companion to man. With the diversities of both horses and man, the two have grown to enjoy the variety of horse sports we all know today. Some people use the "sporting horse" for competition, while many others enjoy this modern equine for pleasure and trail riding. The horse's versatility allows virtually any person, young and old, terrific enjoyment. Furthermore, the reality of the equality of the genders becomes so profound in these horse sports, where men and women are judged equally. We've come a long way baby!

The relationship between women and horses strengthens even further. In the modern day it is no longer acceptable to "break the spirit" of the horse through force for one's gain. Women understand that all too well. The woman has never been able to force an animal of that size and strength to do anything. She has always had to use her intuitive instincts of communication without force, to achieve her goal. To that end, the woman would try to communicate with a partnership language, rather than the predator/prey relationship nature deemed appropriate. To an aside, there are certainly many examples of the male's communication with the horse without force. However, in most of those cases, it is the more experienced horseman that comes to realize the benefits of the partnership relationship.

I recently heard a wonderful saying that for me sums it up. That is, "A man's brain is bigger than his heart. But, a horse's heart is bigger than his brain." It certainly made me think how important and fragile our relationship with the horse can be.

I am certain you will enjoy Jane's writings as I have. I have never considered myself a female activist. However, as I read her words, I realize that the platform

Photo courtesy of Karen O'Connor

At the age of 38, Karen and her mount Biko rode to silver medal honors at the 1996 summer Olympic Games in Atlanta. Karen and her husband David made Olympic history as the first husband and wife to receive medals in the summer games. Biko was named "Eventing Horse of the Century" by the United States Eventing Association.

from which I send my message is not a podium to talk about equal rights issues, rather it is on my horse that I can truly express myself. Ironically, that journey has led me to travel all over the world with my four-legged friends. Ultimately, it has led me back to the podium, the Olympic podium. I am privileged to participate in the only Olympic sport where men and women are judged equally.

The touch and smell of a horse is difficult to describe. I cannot imagine where my life would have been without him. It is my life with horses that has given me clarity. I am an ordinary person allowed to experience extraordinary moments with the horse. Some of these moments, like the Olympic Games, are very public. While others are so private that they are only shared between you and your horse. Those are the ones I cherish the most. Those are the moments that have shaped my life. I love saying, "Show me your horse and I will show you who you are." Because after all for me, when the glitter dies, I'll end up back from where I started my competitive journey, that is, to continue to learn the language of the horse.

Karen O'Connor

INTRODUCTION

For many women, the decision to first pursue riding is the fulfillment of a lifelong dream. The challenge life offers each of us is the determination to be the person we were meant to be. My personal pursuit is an excellent case in point: I have ridden for years, but took my first formal riding lesson at the age of 46. I ferried my youngest child from horse show to horse show for nearly a decade, but did not participate in my first show until the age of 48.

Realizing that the instant you use such words as first, last, only, and best, while stirring never and always into the mix, you, the author, have allowed yourself to be placed in a stewing pot of correction, rebuttal, and verbal dispute. In any group of "horse people" there will be opinions, on any subject related to horses, equal to the number in the group. However, through diligent research, I have tried to assemble an overall view of the history of the woman equestrian, the evolution of the horse, and how the two work together as one. Using my own amateur experiences, I have conveyed my thoughts, feelings, and opinions on the day-to-day benefits of riding, competition, and horsemanship for the total woman.

There are books already on the shelves written for the sole purpose of teaching children and adults "how to" ride, but to my knowledge, none has been written specifically for the female. The history of famous, as well as infamous, equestrians can be found in many volumes, but none chronicles the development of the woman rider from her humble beginnings to her present stature.

So, what are the benefits of a book written specifically for women equestrians? The female is a very complex creature. General books on how to ride would be helpful in understanding the basic concepts of riding, but they would not address the issues that are unique to our gender. Yes, the trot is the trot, and one's sex cannot alter that fact. However, the internal "voices" a woman hears, if left unanswered, can alter her performance in the ring, as well as in life.

All equestrians must maintain physical balance when riding a horse, but women in particular need *balance* in their everyday lives. It is important for women, therefore, to frequently look at their lives and review their chosen paths. The physical benefits gained from riding are obvious ones. However, the emotional, mental, and spiritual growth realized from this sport reaches far beyond understanding.

Riding is an exhilarating sport that sends a charge of excitement coursing through your body. The personal awareness developed in the ring will serve you well in your "other" life. Equally, the bond you create with your horse and your "barn buddies," while rarely understood by the outside world, will enrich your life beyond measure.

I sincerely hope you enjoy the read and cherish the ride!

SECTION ONE
A HISTORY OF THE WOMAN EQUESTRIAN

Before embarking on our personal journey to learn to ride, it is essential to first take a look back at the lives of some of the women who traveled before us. Only by passing through the window of time can we fully appreciate the contribution made by women equestrians of the past to the female riders of today. Women have evolved from mere passengers on horseback to navigators of Olympic mounts. For centuries the lives of women and horses have been interwoven, creating a tapestry of hopes, dreams, and accomplishments. History is the cornerstone of our present and the key to our future.

A HISTORY OF THE WOMAN EQUESTRIAN

Oh sure, occasionally we dream about being an equestrian of Olympic status, but it is usually while spreading peanut butter on a fragile slice of bread. As we fold the clean, fragrant sheets and a seemingly unending pile of socks (which, by the way, never seems to come out evenly), the notion of being "the woman equestrian," drifts in and out of our dream-like state of consciousness. The reality of our lives and where we really want to be in our riding is fortunately much more attainable.

Most of us find ourselves sharing our lives with a collection of other wonderful human beings. With this shared existence comes a multitude of responsibilities, all of which demand a great deal of time and attention. As women, we are constantly giving to others, but unfortunately rarely attend to our own needs. Indeed, time for ourselves is critical, and society, at least those who recognize the merits of equestrian riding, has provided women the time and leisure with which to pursue this noble sport.

History has recorded many women riding horses both for pleasure and necessity. For centuries, participation in equestrian sports has been of immense value for women, both mentally and physically. Listening to one's inner self and disregarding public opinion has fortunately withstood the test of time for female equestrians.

In earlier times, only women of royal blood were privileged enough to have access to horses. Over the centuries, however, more and more women from all walks of life have been able to take up the sport and compete successfully. Riding can give us a much-deserved escape from the day-to-day drudgeries of life. The dryer will still run even if we are not at home to watch the clothes tumble. Crockpots are wonderful inventions that, when properly filled, can produce a dinner fit for royalty. Time reserved for ourselves is essential in our hectic and fractured world that is today. Remember, the flight attendant always instructs you to take care of yourself before assisting your children. There is a reason for that specific order of attention. You are of little good to anyone else if you have not first attended to your personal needs.

Taking a brief look into the history of the female equestrian and the women who acted as the catalysts for change in the sport is a worthwhile endeavor. All equestrians, regardless of sex, share a deep love for horses. These wonderfully giving animals have shared a tremendous part of human life for thousands of years. Thankfully, early art of the fifth century, as well as works from the medieval period, have been well-preserved

From the book The World of Polo, Past and Present *by J.N.P. Watson.*

Anne of Bohemia

showing us that women once rode wearing long skirts riding astride, often carrying infants and bundles, or even engaging in polo-like games. Not until the fifteenth century did women begin to sit sideways on their horses for purposes of slow-moving processionals and other occasions of celebration. This was also the time when someone decided it was not particularly "ladylike" for women to ride at all.

History gives credit to Anne of Bohemia (1366-1394), Queen consort to Richard II of England, for introducing the earliest version of a practical sidesaddle. It was a chair-like invention, based on a pack saddle to which was fitted, usually on the nearside, a wooden footrest, called a planchette. This addition was no doubt added to help aid with balance since women riders sat at a right angle to the horse, and could, therefore, rest their feet on the platform. For additional security, there was a horn or pommel at the front of the saddle that she could hold in the right hand. Riding using this type of saddle rendered women to be not much more than passengers and a groom often led them.

Women were also required to dress as fashion dictated in the elaborate gowns of the time, and the proper etiquette was to be ever present in their style of riding. The idea of women being too weak or easily "damaged" made riding astride even less acceptable in the sixteenth century. Not all women adopted the sidesaddle. There were women who refused to surrender to societal stigmas and continued to hunt riding astride sporting their tall boots and long, divided skirts.

Women in the hunt field took on a much different look from the ones seen today. A foxhunt was an all-day affair. Often the hours passed slowly and there was very little jumping involved. Not only did women have to contend with the required etiquette of the age such as extremely uncomfortable saddles and the masking of their ankles; they were also subject to the ever-growing societal opinion that women were creatures of domesticity. Inevitably, the "a woman's place is in the home" mind-set became even stronger over time.

Catherine de Medici

Up until the late 1700s and into the early nineteenth century, equitation training for women was nonexistent. Hunting was considered an inappropriate and irreputable pastime for women, so their manner of riding was inconsequential. Ironically, just 300 years earlier, the chase was considered to be "a school in life and character" in which many women took part. One such woman of the early Renaissance was Catherine de Medici. Born in Florence, Italy, in 1519, she made significant contributions to riding for all women. After taking several hard falls while on the hunt, Catherine must have paused to review why she had lost her seat and what could be done to prevent a recurrence. She made important modifications to the physical placement of the female rider in the saddle as well as to the saddle itself. She began to sit facing in a more forward direction, hooking her right leg around the pommel of the saddle. She went a step further by adding an extra horn on the near side of her saddle so as to secure her right knee and help keep her small frame on her horse.

Catherine was not always so confident in regard to herself or her abilities. It was outward appearance that rendered her quite insecure and, eventually, made her strong. At the tender age of 14, Catherine was betrothed to the Duke of Orleans, who was to become the next King of France, Henry II. Realizing that she was, at best, sadly plain, had eyes much too large for her face, and stood not quite five feet tall, this tiny young girl was terrified at the thought of going before the likes of the French Court.

Finding herself lacking the help of adoring mice and an overindulgent fairy godmother, Catherine turned to an inventive Florentine artisan whose name has been lost with time. It was the intention of this gifted craftsman to divert all attention from Catherine's face and turn Paris on its heels by dazzling high society with an incredible gown and something else quite inventive. An unforgettable dress was a snap to create, but how to get Catherine above the crowd, so to speak, was the bigger question.

On September 1, 1533, Catherine de Medici said good-bye to her beloved Florence and made her way to Paris. The wedding was even more grand than she had imagined and all of Paris clamored to meet her. It was not until the Royal Ball, however, that they would get their chance.

As she entered the grand ballroom, all eyes were on Catherine. The men were said to have been staggered by her sensuous beauty, and women were held breathless with envy. There was something in the way she moved, an unusual sway, a walk the French had never before seen. What could it be? The gift given by the forgotten Italian artisan to this plain, tiny, and unattractive girl was the first pair of high-heeled shoes, proving once again the lengths to which women have been forced to go to render themselves visually acceptable.

Throughout her life Catherine de Medici remained truly devoted to riding, but always dressed in eye-catching attire. Her clothes had sheltered her from the embarrassment of her outward appearance since her youth, so why not carry this security blanket over to her riding? If society was determined to inflict such strict rules of etiquette upon the female equestrian, Catherine's addition to her wardrobe spoke volumes about their determination. The sidesaddle design de Medici created, although less secure than the modern version, became the standard for over 200 years.

History tells us that Queen Isabella of Spain, born in Madrigal de las Altas Torres, on April 22, 1451, though

Queen Isabella

not thought to be a particularly nice person, was an incredible cross-country rider. Her abilities would match up in spirit and talent with any female endurance rider of today, remembering also that Queen Isabella rode sidesaddle, which, at the time, lacked even the second horn of de Medici. With her politically troubled nation in turmoil, Isabella once set out on a very long, grueling journey over the Spanish countryside. This is another glimpse into the independence of history's women, their quiet refusal to accept someone else's word as fact, and their determination to ride regardless of public opinion. The reality that Catherine braved the dangers of war in support of her country was said to have inspired her loyal troops.

Queen Isabella was somewhat of a visionary in the area of selective breeding of horses. Years later, she established a stud farm in Andalusia and gave her name to the cream-colored horses calling them "Isobels." The care given by humankind of the past to careful breeding practices of horses has contributed to the quality animals we enjoy today.

Born on November 2, 1755, in Vienna, Austria, Marie Antoinette, one of history's most famous women, was an excellent equestrian both riding astride and aside. She only began to ride sidesaddle after she became the Queen of France by marrying Louis XVI.

During the first years of their marriage, Marie Antoinette was criticized for many indiscretions such as gambling, sleigh racing, opera balls, and hunting in the Bois de Boulogne. While all of this, and probably much more, did occur it was mostly attributed to the fact that she was so unhappy at home. Due to a childhood illness, her husband, Louis XVI, was unable to consummate their marriage for the first seven years. To fill her lonely days and nights, Marie found the company of others comforting. This choice did not win her favor with the people of France however. Equally, the citizens of the monarchy were unaware of King Louis' physical disorder and blamed the "no children" status of the royal couple on Marie Antoinette.

A flamboyant character, to say the least, Marie Antoinette defied the female social dress code and rode as she pleased, sporting tall boots, breeches, an elaborate plumed hat and a gold lace jabot (a cascade of frills down the front of a shirt). She went a step further by tossing such things as a leopard skin over her saddle for instant panache. Her infamous "cake" comment, which some historians argue was never said, proved to be quite unfortunate, but no one could argue with her ability to ride. Surely she must have wondered, "Where can a girl find a fast horse when she needs to get out of town?"

Lady Godiva's famous ride, short as it was, has truly stood the test of time. Unfortunately, there is no actual record of her birth or death, but we know she lived in England during the 1000s, most probably as an adult from 1040-1080. Wife to the Earl Leofric of Mercia, Lady Godiva (Godgifu, as it was originally spelled), history has it, asked her husband to lower the heavy taxes he had imposed on the citizens as Lord of Coventry. He agreed to make an adjustment to the taxes if she would agree to ride *au naturel* through the market area of the township. One would hope he loved his wife and made the wager trusting she would never accept such a challenge. But Lady Godiva's convictions for fair play and the people of her township outweighed any personal embar-

Lady Godiva

rassment. She made only one request of the villagers, asking that they remain inside and keep their blinds closed. So incredibly grateful to Lady Godiva for her internal strength and outward willingness to help them during desperate times, all of the townspeople agreed to do as she wished.

According to many artists' renderings, clothed only by her long hair, Lady Godiva climbed atop her horse and was led through the streets of town. However, in one of the earliest surviving chronicles of her ride, Roger of Wendover (died, 1236), wrote an account of the famous event dated 1057. Lady Godiva was a very accomplished horsewoman who also enjoyed the spirited hunt. These early notations suggest that she sat astride in the saddle with an air of composure and dignity for that historic ride. It is also written that she did not travel alone, but was accompanied by two properly clothed female equestrians riding one on either side and slightly behind. Ancient records also show that around 1057 there were no taxes levied in Coventry on human residents; horses yes, but not people. These entries support the notion that Leofric was apparently a man of his word.

According to a later story, a tailor named Tom could not resist the temptation and peeped through a shutter as Lady Godiva rode by. As history, or legend, would have it, he was instantly struck blind, and as a result this incident is said to be the origin of the phrase "peeping Tom." In appreciation to her, up until the late 1800s, a procession was held at different intervals to celebrate Lady Godiva's courage.

The pen is mightier than the sword is a phrase, that has been used for centuries. It has perhaps never been quite as true as in the world of horses. These glorious animals have been used as beasts of burden since they grew large enough to support the physical weight of humankind.

There is one particular lady who deserves an enormous round of applause and our sincere appreciation for her efforts to right the wrongs created by society in the treatment of horses. Anna Sewell scribed a book in the 1870s that did more for the prevention of cruelty to animals than any other work to date. There have been over 30 million copies of *Black Beauty* sold since its debut. This gripping story has been translated into most languages and made into motion pictures. It is thought to be the most read and loved animal story of all time.

Photo courtesy of David Watkins

Anna Sewell

Born in 1820, Anna spent most of her younger years alongside her mother in a basement kitchen in the inner city of London. There was little joy or delight to her days, with one exception, that being when she and her mother would take the bruised apples across the street and feed them to the carriage horses standing in wait for their next fare. Anna was always deeply hurt by the lack of care and concern given to these horses.

Over the summer months, Anna traveled to Buxton to visit other members of her family. Her uncle had one particular horse, Balsam, whom she loved to ride. She worked hard developing her skills, but with a gentle voice, not a heavy hand. Anna understood that it was not necessary to use force when dealing with these marvelous creatures.

During one of these visits to her uncle's farm, she suffered a severe sprain to either her knee or her ankle, which one is not exactly clear. In any event, the injury was debilitating enough to render her lame and in constant pain. As the years passed, Anna became confined to the interior of her London home, but spent hours in front of the window watching the horse-drawn carriages as they passed by. Her heart shattered as she watched the overworked and undernourished once-grand animals strain to pull carts made much too heavy. She flinched as the stylish ladies of the Victorian time drove their horses using bearing reins. This cruel piece of tack forced the horse to hold his head high in the air and rise on his hind legs with front hooves cutting the air. Bearing reins made it difficult for the horse to pull a carriage, as he naturally would do, by lowering his head and using his shoulders. This dreadful piece of equipment also made it difficult for the horse to breathe normally. Cab horses and livery horses were forced to endure this treatment as well.

Once published, this wonderful book, *Black Beauty*, caused quite a stir among British veterinarians and humanitarians alike. Within several years, the use of the bearing rein was abolished completely. Humane societies and animal rights groups sprang up as a result of her work as well.

Anna Sewell died at the age of 58 from complications her physicians were never able to diagnose. Her death came about a year after the publication of her famous story. It is interesting to note that the horses being used to draw the hearse that carried her body, were dressed in bearing reins. Anna's mother would not allow this outlawed tack to be used and insisted that the owner of the hearse remove the forbidden reins.

There has perhaps never been one work or person who has affected so many people and done so much for horses as Anna Sewell and her book *Black Beauty*. This story has caused otherwise disinterested people to sit up and pay attention to the world they share with animals and how those creatures are treated. What a lasting tribute to the caring heart of Anna Sewell.

Although riding became mainly a pastime for wealthy women of noble birth, there is one exception who stands out. British courtesan (a prostitute or kept woman who associates with men of rank of wealth) Catherine Walters was born in the back streets of Liverpool, but used her natural abilities and instinct to become an expert rider. Her riding talents enabled her to cross the very strict class boundaries of the nineteenth century, even if it was as a lady of questionable character and intention. Catherine's life was a study of Victorian morals, one of which was in that day it was acceptable to solicit in Hyde Park while on horseback, but not if on foot. An area of London known as "Rotten Row" provided a plentiful buffet of rich and stylish gentlemen.

Catherine was, however, quite selective in the men she chose. Upon arriving in London, around the age of 20, she became the mistress of several well-to-do men. It was a requirement of Catherine's to enjoy the company of the men with whom she shared her time and affections. One of her gentlemen friends, the poet Wilfrid Blunt, had the pleasure of her company for just a few hours, but the memory of that experience found its way into his writings for many years to come.

Walters was hired by the owners of a local livery stable to show off their mounts. She attracted so much attention when riding that she halted traffic during London's rush hour, not because she was a prostitute, but because she had the ability to hold her audience captive. Beautiful as well as a very accomplished horsewoman, Catherine, or "Skittles" as she was called, introduced the elegant silk hat and veil for riding. She was known for her style and never displayed any sign of vulgarity in her manner of dress or in her behavior. It would seem that women have always taken on an attitude of looking good while riding. Perhaps it was because so few women rode in centuries past that they attracted a great deal of attention to themselves and to their chosen attire.

Catherine "Skittles" Walters died in September 1920 in South Street, Mayfair, somewhat a recluse, but remembered for her loving and caring heart.

The invention that revolutionized sidesaddle riding and brought such women as Elisabeth, "Sisi", Empress of Austria, born on Christmas, 1837, in Munich, Bavaria, one of the nineteenth century's most renowned and royal equestrian women, to the forefront of cross-country riding, was the "leaping head." In 1830, an otherwise obscure Parisian riding master, Jules Charles Pellier, designed a sidesaddle containing a third pommel placed below the other two. The leaping head, as this additional pommel was called, screwed into the saddle tree and curved outward over the rider's left thigh. The top pommel was soon discarded and the rider was able to sit in a much more secure position. Women could now jump fences without the fear of falling, as was the case with the former saddle containing two upright pommels.

Elisabeth recognized the need for a rider's body to harmonize with the motion of the horse over the fences. Before this time women rode with a more rigid and upright seat simply to maintain their balance in the saddle. Equitation had not been stressed in regard to women's riding style due to the fact that it was nearly impossible to achieve using the old sidesaddle. With her dazzling riding talents and immaculate dress, into which she literally had to be sewn, the Empress attracted hundreds of onlookers to watch her hunt during a visit to Britain and Ireland. Empress Elisabeth's corseted clothing was so tight that when she was assassinated in 1898, by Italian anarchist Luigi Luccheni in Geneva, Switzerland, she was initially unaware she had been fatally wounded.

In keeping with her fierce personal discipline, Elisabeth practiced, using the Austrian steeplechase courses, for long hours on mastery of the sidesaddle. With the death of her son in 1889, her dearest cousin's passing just three years before, and an empty marriage, Elisabeth was very unhappy at home and used riding as one means of being absent from home for long periods of time. Elisabeth also suffered from anorexia. Again, riding served a purpose, that purpose being one of intense exercise so as to keep her frame painfully thin. The diets and overexercising to which she subjected her body very probably did her more harm than good.

Over the years, English hunting had evolved from the slow and uneventful days of years past, to a flat-out pace requiring more skill and better equitation. Her expertise in the hunt field, while on "sporting tours" in England and Ireland, earned Elisabeth the reputation of being a fearless horsewoman. Her abilities, and the invention of a more secure sidesaddle, helped defuse gender prejudice and opened the way for women to return to the sport and participate on a more equal basis.

Another female equestrian, Johanna July, was born in the 1850s to a family of Seminole Indians and freed African-American slaves. This group of settlers left Florida in 1842 at the end of the Seminole War and resettled in northern Mexico. They would move one more time in 1871 making Eagle Pass, Texas, their final home. Johanna's family went to work for the U.S. Army removing troublesome Indians from the U.S. side of the Rio Grande, and in payment, was given a tract of land at Brackettville.

Johanna was taught to ride as a young girl by an old pioneer named Adam Wilson. She preferred to ride bareback, which requires excellent balance, and used only a rope around the horse's neck, as opposed to a bridle. Johanna became quite famous throughout the area as an expert horsewoman who wore strings of beads, gold earrings, and very colorful clothes. After her father died and her brother moved away, Johanna had to support herself and earned a living as a horse breaker. She tamed wild horses for soldiers at nearby Fort Duncan. She would ride the horses into the Rio Grande making them stand in the river until they calmed down. Nervous at being in the water, most of the horses would listen to Johanna's commands when they were allowed to return to dry land.

Johanna was married to a Seminole scout for a brief period, but did not enjoy domestic life and yearned to be with her horses. Leaving her husband, she returned to her mother's home near the Rio Grande.

Isabella Bird (1831-1904), eldest daughter of English clergyman Edward Bird, grew up in Tattenhall, Cheshire. As a young girl she suffered from a spinal disorder, along with depression and various other infirmities. In 1854, at the age of 23, she was encouraged by her physician to consider an extensive ocean voyage to America and Canada in hopes of improving her health. Isabella found the sea air of the transatlantic expedition to be quite invigorating and she very much enjoyed her first taste of freedom. Soon after her return to England, her beloved father passed away.

Isabella led a somewhat quiet life during the 1860s with her mother and sister but longed to return to her life of adventure. In 1873, she reached the Rocky Mountains of the United States by way of a trip to Australia and Hawaii. Upon arriving in America's Wild West, she found an untamed world exploding with unharnessed individuals. Colorado was, at that time, outside of the Union. The railroads were not yet complete, and the law was in question on a day-by-day basis. Isabella found her way to an area of Colorado known as Estes Park. While in the park, she filled her days with 10-hour day trips on horseback and made numerous attempts at mountain climbing, however unsuccessful. In letters to her sister, Henrietta, Isabella wrote of the

beauty of the American West. She also spoke, in somewhat cryptic style, of an emotional involvement she
shared with a man by the name of Jim Nugent.

Isabella made an incredible ride of 500 miles on horseback through Colorado. She crossed the Arkansas Divide at an elevation of almost 8,000 feet, traversed the
Western Continental Divide soaring to around 12,000
feet, and spent part of a day with a gentleman by the
name of "Comanche Bill," who proved to be no gentleman at all. He was said to have killed Indians in an
effort to avenge the murder of a family member slain in
an earlier massacre.

Despite their often petite and somewhat fragile appearance, equestrian women of the past were as determined, skilled, and devoted to horses as any woman of
today. We owe these women a debt of gratitude for
refusing to surrender their love of riding or compro-
mise their beliefs.

Times have certainly changed; riding is no longer
enjoyed only by the rich and famous. Today people from
all walks of life can enjoy riding. Finally, women are
judged on an equal basis and no allowance is given to
compensate for gender. In Olympic competition, for
example, there is only one sport in which men and
women compete on a completely equal basis, and that
is riding. In the equestrian venue, there is no difference
in size or weight of equipment, distances, or time of
completion in regard to event.

Women first competed with men in dressage in the
Helsinki Olympics in 1952. Lis Hartel was the lady who
put women on the map in the arena of female Olympic
equestrians. This was an incredible feat due to the fact
that she had to retrain herself to ride after recovering
from polio. Lis went on to earn the silver medal for
Denmark in this event.

Karen O'Connor was another such equestrian Olym-
piad who was quite successful in the 2000 games held

U.S.Olympic Equestrian Team of 2000: L.auren Hough, Laura Kraut, Margie Goldstein-Engle, and Nona Garson. Photos courtesy of Chronicle of the Horse, call 1-800-877-5467 to subscribe.

in Sydney, Australia. She, aboard Prince Panache, owned by Jacqueline Mars, rode to the third-best score of the dressage phase of the Olympic three-day event. This moved the U.S. Equestrian Team (USET) into the third position going into the cross-country segment of competition. The three-day team finished the games with a bronze medal for the United States.

The 2000 games were also the first time the United States had sent an all-female show-jumping team. This team included Lauren Hough, Laura Kraut, Margie Goldstein-Engle, and Nona Garson.

Women have also found success in the discipline of horse racing as well. The first recorded woman jockey was Alicia Maynell of England. She took the irons in her first competition in a four-mile race in York, England, in 1804. In 1934, Mary Hirsch became the first licensed female trainer of thoroughbred racehorses. Diane Crump was the first female jockey to ride in the Kentucky Derby in 1970. Julie Krone is perhaps the most famous woman jockey winning the Belmont Stakes aboard Colonial Affair in 1993. Julie retired from racing in 1999 as the all-time winningest female jockey with over 3,000 victories. In the year 2000, she was named to the Thoroughbred Racing's Hall of Fame. To date, she is the only woman to have achieved this honor.

Sandra Day O'Connor, the first female Justice of the U.S. Supreme Court, was born in El Paso, Texas, and grew up on her family's remote Arizona and New Mexico cattle ranch. Ms. O'Connor learned to shoot and ride before she was eight years old. After attending Stanford Law School, she went on to serve as the Arizona assistant attorney general. Later, Sandra Day O'Connor was appointed to a vacant seat of the Arizona State Senate, was elected Superior Court judge, and appointed to the Arizona Court of Appeals. President Ronald Reagan nominated her as the first female member of the United States Supreme Court in 1981, making Ms. O'Connor the 102nd justice of America's highest court.

In 2002, Justice O'Connor led five inductees, including herself, into the National Cowgirl Museum's Hall of Fame. She was given the honor of cutting the ceremonial ribbon, after which she received her medal. In addition to Justice O'Connor, four other outstanding women were inducted into the Cowgirl Hall of Fame: Polly Burson, who has been called one of the premier stuntwomen in Hollywood history; Kathy Daughn, one of the top cutting horse competitors in the country, Arlene Kensinger; a trick rider and barrel racer who created the Cheyenne Quadrillettes (an equestrian drill-team) as well as the Cheyenne Frontier Days Dandies; and Anne Burnett Tandy, a founder of the American Quarter Horse Association and generous philanthropist.

History has documented that women will ride regardless of societal, financial, or physical restrictions. The love equestrian women possess for their sport and for the horses they ride has withstood the test of time. Breaking down the barriers inflicted upon women has been a long and sometimes, painful journey, but one met head on with conviction and determination. The joy realized from riding has no measure, nor can the love of those glorious animals called horses be explained. It just is!

SECTION TWO
THE FEMALE EQUESTRIAN

When making the deci-sion to learn to ride, you should give careful atten-tion to the order in which your choices are arranged. In the opinion of this au-thor, choosing an instruc-tor is of number one im-portance. It is imperative that there be a clear line of communication and mu-tual understanding be-tween you and your trainer. Everything else will easily find its place if this key ingredient is given

Taylor Slaughter studies the course

top priority. Your basic riding apparel should be number two on your list. No one should ever be allowed on a horse without an approved safety helmet. Good paddock boots are also quite necessary. Understanding just what to expect from your first lessons is important as well. Having your expectations set too high initially can prove shattering when the reality of your first lessons sets in. Choosing a stable will only be important when you are the proud owner of your own horse. Try to relax, enjoy each riding day, and be patient with yourself.

THE FEMALE
EQUESTRIAN

Choosing an Instructor

From the time of the introductions, take note of your initial reaction to the person who may become your trainer. Were you at ease when talking to this person? Did he or she welcome you with a smile and the feeling that he or she had nothing else to do but talk with you, or did you get the impression that you were in the way? You are planning to put a great deal of trust and money in the hands of this person, so what happens during this "first meeting" really does matter.

If you are a parent shopping for an instructor for your child, wait to hear some discussion of safety, rules, and barn manners. If those three things are not discussed in the first fifteen minutes of your initial meeting, LEAVE! Nothing is more important to parents than their child's safety, happiness, and well-being. All good trainers will begin their speech entitled, "How I Run My Barn," by listing their top ten concerns or rules. Safety, cooperation, fun, manners, and respect for others should all be at the top of that list.

When looking for a compatible trainer, adults searching for a teaching barn should expect nothing less for themselves. It is sometimes a bit more difficult for adults to mesh into a new environment, so have patience when looking around. Adults also come equipped with preconceived notions of how they would do "it." Remember, you are the one looking for a teaching barn, not the trainer. Most of the time you will know right away if you and the instructor will be able to get along with one another.

There must also be an open line of communication between you, the rider, and your trainer. Not understanding what is being said or asked of you can cause a variety of problems, some of which can cause serious injury. If you feel that there is a lack of caring or concern on the part of your instructor, there probably is. I suggest you address your concerns and if nothing changes, you should probably part company.

What to Wear

No matter what your age, you must always wear an approved safety helmet when you ride! This is not open for discussion or debate. If the instructor at your barn does not require helmets, then you should change stables and the trainer should be shot. Approved helmets are expensive, but aren't you, not to mention your child, worth the price? Your local tack shop will have several brands to choose from, and you really must try them on to get a proper fit.

The next necessity is a good pair of boots. You don't need a pair of tall boots to start, but you really do need a good pair of paddock boots. Riding boots are made to support your ankles, protect your toes, and have a heel to keep your foot from slipping through the stirrup. The pair you choose should be the one that best fits your foot. In this area, looks should have little to nothing to do with your selection.

Riding breeches come in a multitude of designs, colors, and styles. Again, this is a personal choice. Your trainer may frown at zebra striped pants, but they do exist. Comfort is very important when choosing any riding clothes. In the middle of a lesson you cannot hop off your horse and go change your clothes because your pants are too tight, bunching up, or falling off. Whether you are buying breeches for yourself or your child, I suggest you not spend a great deal of money on every-day riding clothes. Riding is a dirty sport, and your clothes will take a beating.

Most any sort of polo shirt or T- shirt will do for daily lessons in the warmer months. Occasionally, a trainer will have a specific shirt style he or she prefers, and if that is the case, he or she should tell you before you purchase anything. During the colder months you will need clothes that layer. As you warm up during a lesson, you will want to be able to remove the outer layer. When trying on clothes, layer them in the store. For example, the outermost layer, a coat or jacket, must comfortably fit over a sweater and a turtleneck allowing you to move freely while riding.

There are a wide variety of "extras" you can purchase and I suggest you wait a while on these things. My reason for asking you to wait is so you can avoid impulse purchasing. After you have a handful of lessons under your belt, you will have a better understanding of what you need and want in the way of additional accessories.

Riding gloves help you grip the reins while protecting your hands. The cotton variety will allow your hands to breathe and will not become slick when wet. However, if you plan to show, you must also have a pair of black leather gloves.

Chaps are very nice, but are also quite pricey. You can wear half-chaps or purchase a full-length set of leather chaps. This is a personal choice and one you will not want to rush into.

If you are a parent outfitting a child, your child will want what everyone else has. For girls between the ages of eight and 18, different is a disaster and what to wear is paramount in their minds. This does not mean that you are a bad parent if you refuse to pay two hundred dollars for a raincoat. It does mean that you are sure to hear about it, a lot! I would suggest that you set down some ground rules before your first shopping excursion. Most of us live on a budget, and there are limits to what we can afford. With this in mind, be honest with your child. Tell her how much you can spend. Most children appreciate your honesty and will cooperate. It is also ridiculous to buy lots of clothes for a child who will surely outgrow them before she wears them out.

When outfitting children for a horse show, they really must be properly dressed. The judge will subtract points if a child is incorrectly outfitted. Again you do not have to purchase the most expensive clothes. There are many affordable, and equally correct, show clothes on the market for the growing child. Many stables have a stepladder range of children at their barn. Before you go shopping, ask if any of the older children have outgrown clothes they wish to sell or lend out. Additionally, most tack shops have a "gently used" section of show clothes to choose from as well.

The same can be said for the adult rider in regard to sensible purchasing of clothing. Buying the minimum to begin with and adding to your collection a bit at a time is, in my opinion, the way to go. Most women will quickly find the brand and style that just fits their body shape and pocketbook. Your geographical location also plays a huge part in your riding wardrobe. Also, your chosen discipline makes a difference as well. Each discipline has its individual set of clothes both for you and your horse.

Relax and give yourself time to assess the situation. Comfort and freedom of movement are the primary goals in your decision-making process. Try very hard not to allow yourself to be talked into something you really do not want or that is not comfortable. That purchase will waste a good deal of your money, die of dry-rot, and find its place in the "what was I thinking" section of your closet.

The Young Rider's First Lesson

The first few lessons will probably consist of learning how to tack-up your pony, groom your mount, and get off and on the pony. All of these things are very important first steps. Don't ever ride a pony or horse without wearing your approved helmet and having adult supervision!

Tacking up your pony is a key ingredient to a successful first ride. Make sure to pay close attention to what is being said to you about which saddle and bridle to use. Also, ask for your first attempts at tacking-up to be checked for accuracy before mounting (getting on) the pony. A girth that is too loose will find you on the ground and the pony running free around the property. Equally, an ill-fitting bridle will only aggravate the pony, and one should never aggravate a pony.

Notice I have said pony, not horse. You will ride a mount that is more suited to your individual size. As you grow, your trainer will put you on a larger pony and eventually you will be tall enough to ride a horse. Ponies are divided into three categories: small, medium, and large. For example, if you were around the age of five, your trainer would place you on a small pony. This would insure your being able to correctly use your natural aids (your legs, hands, and seat).

Grooming your pony is done before and after you ride. There is no excuse for not doing your very best job! Remember, this animal has worked hard for you and he deserves the best care you can give. Improper grooming of his coat can cause a pony to develop body sores and other skin problems. Not picking out his feet can result in lameness or sore feet. Returning a dirty, wet, or hot pony to his stall can cause serious problems and may even be fatal in some cases. If you ever "for-

Photo by Jane Slaughter

Maggie Hunt with "Peter Pumpkin"

get" to properly care for the pony you have been given to ride, you can count on your trainer strongly "reminding" you to never do that again.

Your ring work will concentrate on the walk at first and finding your balance. You will work up to the trot and eventually the canter. It will sometimes be difficult for you to be patient during a lesson. You will feel that you are ready to move on, but you must always listen to your trainer. The basics are your most important lessons. Once you have those first skills firmly rooted in your mind, you can move on to the harder "stuff."

Don't forget your manners! Be nice, clean up after yourself AND especially, behind your pony, and patiently wait your turn. No one likes a know-it-all, and riding is supposed to be fun. Competition helps you improve by making you work a little harder. Nanny, nanny, booboo is not competition, it is being rude. Before you leave the barn for the day, remember to say thank you to your instructor and your pony. The pony would probably enjoy a kiss on the nose, a soft pat on the neck, and a carrot too.

The Novice Mature Rider

Riding can do more for your physical and mental "self" than you could ever imagine. It is a wonderful form of physical exercise for your entire body and an intense brain stimulant as well. As we mature, women have to struggle with the issues of bone density, weight management, and mental clarity. Riding can help with all of these concerns and more.

I would define a novice mature rider as a woman over the age of 40. Do you remember looking into the mirror on your 40th birthday? Me too. Yikes! Lots of water has run under that bridge, but there is still lots more water to go before you call it quits. With that in mind, I would suggest you begin with a realistic approach to your quest to ride. You do not plan to "go for the gold," nor do you have any intentions of going on tour. You just want to learn to ride correctly, have a good time, and be with people who share your love for horses.

Choosing the correct stable and trainer is paramount. You are not five years old and thus require a trainer who can teach to your specific needs. Most mature women are juggling a job and a family, while trying to fulfill their own needs. The last thing you need is an instructor who does not understand where you are coming from. From time to time, your trainer will raise his or her voice in your direction. This elevation of tone is to gain your immediate attention to a specific instruction. Yelling for the purpose of humiliation, however, is totally unacceptable and should never be directed toward you. Instructors who are constantly screaming at or verbally degrading their students need counseling and a career change.

As a beginning rider it is important to understand that you will very probably be riding with children who are also beginners. If you are employed, then your only lesson time option is in the afternoon or evening. That is also the case for children who are in school. Don't let this keep you from charging full-speed ahead. I love my lessons with kids. Children are fun to be with, generally they enjoy having a "mom" type around, and most children think it is unbelievable that this old lady can keep up and sometimes kick their butts. You will learn a great deal from these young upstarts and they from you. Children do keep you young and on your toes.

The physical exercise you are engaged in while riding is making you stronger with every lesson. This converts into years added to your life, stronger bones, better circulation, reduced body fat, increased muscle tone, a healthier heart, and looking and feeling FABULOUS! Working out at home, walking, or most any other form of daily exercise will also help your efforts in the ring. Riding is a physically demanding sport and you will need to be in shape to be successful.

Between the ages of 40 and 60, women go through some incredible changes in their physical being as well as their mental self. Not only does riding strengthen the body, it does wonders for the mind. Riding requires constant focus and, therefore, your brain cannot take the day off. You are constantly thinking when you ride by using your natural aids, watching out for the other participants, and listening and reacting to the instructions of your trainer. You are also in constant communication with your horse. This communication is especially nice because horses don't talk back, complain about their supper, or whine about what you want them to wear. Horses are also always glad to see you, they love the attention you lavish upon them, and are willing to work, never asking for an allowance.

Riding is not just good for your mind, it is also good for your soul. If you are a working mother, it is so important to give to yourself as well. Far too often we as women put our needs last. The old phrase, "If mom is happy, everybody is happy" is true. It is your job to see to it that you give yourself some much-needed time. Your family will adjust. They will become more self-sufficient, and, in the process, they will find a deeper appreciation for all you do for them.

Try and relax during your lessons. Remember, this is supposed to be fun. Your trainer will not ask you to do anything more that walk and trot for a good while. Finding your balance in the saddle and your rhythm takes time. If you have questions, ASK. Keeping quiet about things you do not understand will lead to frustration and confusion.

Choosing a Stable

First impressions do matter and especially in regard to choosing a stable. Before deciding on any one riding facility, I strongly suggest that you take the time to shop around.

A barn should be visually neat and tidy any time you visit. It is also a good idea to make at least one unannounced visit. I know this sounds sneaky, but a surprise look-see will allow you to assess how the stable is run on any given day. If you are a parent shopping for an instructional riding facility for your child, cleanliness and attention to safety should be foremost in your mind. The same is true if you are an adult looking to board your horse or for a teaching barn as well.

As you look around the farm, pay close attention to the basic upkeep of the entire area. For example, are the fence railings secure, are the stall and gate latches in good working order, do all of the pastures or paddocks have clean water troughs, do all of the ponies and horses appear to be happy and healthy, is the muck (manure) pile neat and in a central spot away from feed and grazing space?

Thinking in terms of yourself and storage of your personal things, ask to see the tack room, laundry facilities, the office, and lastly, the bathroom. There should be a separate space designated as the tack room. It should be neat and organized and have a door that can be closed to keep out unwanted critters, dust, and dirt. Most barns have a washer and dryer for "horse clothes." This allows each rider to have clean saddle pads, wraps, and towels. It is also another outward sign that the owner of the stable understands the need for cleanliness. There should be an office or lounge where you can use the telephone, have a seat, a refrigerator to store snacks or drinks, a people sink, and perhaps, a television to watch videos taken of you or others riding. Lastly, take a look at the bathroom. If the cobwebs in the corners resemble wall hangings, your shoes stick to the floor, or the only thing left of the toilet seat is its hinges, then perhaps the overall attention to cleanliness is questionable.

Next, look at the riding space itself. Is the ring, either indoor or outside, in good condition? What type of footing is available and, if it is an outdoor ring, is the composition workable in most any weather condition? Is the arena illuminated? If you can only ride in the daylight hours and only on a beautiful day, then this would be a serious downfall in my opinion.

Photo by Branam's Photography

Jane Slaughter and Sailor

All of these things are very important when choosing a barn. If the answer to any of these questions is no, then I suggest you continue to look around.

SECTION THREE
THE FEMININE SELF

The "voices" women hear are very real and must be addressed. Ignoring these internal whispers can alter your performance in the ring as well as in life. Learning to manage your time efficiently and rid your life of unnecessary clutter will reap rewards beyond your expectations. Proper nutrition and exercise will create a healthier and happier you. A quality life has no price tag.

The women who ride at Sandy River Equestrian Center

VOICES: MENTAL & EMOTIONAL

When a young child takes her first riding lesson she enters the ring of the equestrian world, so to speak, free of baggage. Children are so quick to learn and rarely question their instructor or themselves. As the dismissal bell sounds announcing the end of the school day, little girls bounce into the car or bus leaving all of their worries behind. It is only as we age that women seem to carry the weight of the world on our shoulders. Some of our adult troubles can be left at the "door," but others are not so easily set aside. It is those concerns that grasp tenaciously to our mind and soul that need discussion. Knowing you are not alone in this struggle is a comforting thought as well.

THE UNREALISTIC EXPECTATIONS WE ADD TO OUR PLATE

I can't remember how old I was when I first asked for a horse, but I am sure it was before my fifth birthday. Whenever my parents would ask what I would like for any gift-giving occasion, I would always respond with, "A horse, but I know that I cannot have one, so anything will be fine." I was not being a brat; I simply never wanted anything other than a horse of my own.

As most horse lovers of my generation, I grew up watching *National Velvet* and dreamed of riding like Velvet Brown over lush landscape. Every Saturday was spent glued in front of the television watching *My Friend Flicka* and *Fury*. What horse-nut young girl didn't watch Disney's *Swamp Fox* and *Miracle of the White Stallions*? For endless weekend hours we galloped on foot through the neighborhood pretending to ride our own horse who was every bit as good as Velvet Brown's "Pie." None of us ever understood why our fathers refused to surrender the back yard to pasture. Wilbur Post did for *Mr. Ed*, so why wouldn't our dads?

WISHFUL THINKING VS. REALITY

I am not a psychologist and have no credentials in the field of "mental wellness." I do, however, have 32 years of experience in the field of life as an overworked, underpaid, public educator who is also the mother of two. I have figured out how to take care of my personal needs without depriving my family of theirs. Sometimes, simply surviving the day can educate you far beyond your expectations.

Life is a constant battle between what you hoped would happen and what is your actual reality. Like most people who are passionate about their sport, you have fantasized from time to time about riding off into the sunset with Hollywood's latest heartthrob, or excelling to the level of the most current superstar of your sport. Looking across the dinner table, you realize that your chosen mate – wonderful as he is – will never pass for "Little Joe Cartwright" and we could not begin to stop a team of runaway horses without a scratch, as did the women of the silver screen. Life does not supply us with a script nor is there a "Hazel" working in most of our homes. The ebony-clad villains in our lives come dressed as the realization that you cannot win all of the time, you aren't as young as you once were, you will never be everyone's friend, it's OK to say no, and your "non-horse" friends don't really care to listen to you prattle on about your passion.

VOICE NUNBER ONE: DO THESE BREECHES MAKE ME LOOK FAT?

Turning the pages of any equestrian catalogue, the subscriber will find one beautiful woman after another. These women also have the perfect figure, makeup, and look great in their helmets. There is not one hint of cellulite, hips, or midriff bulge. Television, Hollywood, and periodicals have done women a terrible disservice by placing such supreme value on one's outwardly appearance. We are constantly bombarded with ways to stay thin, vanish our wrinkles, and extend our life expectancy. From the time we are young girls, the image of the alleged perfect female has been deeply embedded in our subconscious.

The teenage years are perhaps the worst time for a female in wrestling with the issue of image. "Everyone is watching. Do I look fat in these breeches? He hates me. Nobody likes me!" are all very real concerns of today's young women.

As we age, we still have these worries, but have found ways to coexist with our insecurities. Riding can do more for your mind and soul than you would ever imagine. It is fabulous exercise and a definite confidence builder. Riding promotes self-discipline, a strong work ethic, cooperation, concern for others, and self-esteem to name just a few. All of these qualities are things we want for our children and for ourselves. Once you actually get to the farm, there should be a sign reading: **Before Entering, Please Leave Your Worries at the Gate.**

Remember, you will sweat, you will get dirty, you will make mistakes, you will have your feelings hurt, you will laugh and sometimes cry, but you will also improve with every lesson, both mentally and physically. With improvement comes strength and personal growth.

VOICE NUMBER TWO: COMPETITION IS GOOD..YES?

Competition is a tough one! On the one hand women, by nature, are the peacemakers and caregivers. We spend a lifetime teaching our children how to get along with others and to share, while helping with homework, mending boo boos, broken hearts, and surviving their middle- school years.

Flipping the coin to the other side, the same peacemaker sits in the bleachers quietly praying for her daughter to beat the pants off of every other little girl in the same division. This makes for a tough balance between the Donna Reed, dusting in chiffon and pearls, role model we grew up on and the super teen, vampire slayer image of today's young women. You want your child to try and do her best, but, in her effort to be competitive, she needs to be considerate of others. Children, especially girls, are constantly told to shed their passive skin and stand up for themselves. This is not necessarily bad advice, but you will quickly lose every friend you have if you do not learn to temper your aggression a bit. It is one thing to be assertive; it is then again another to simply be rude and ill-mannered.

It is a fantastic feeling of euphoria when the announcer calls out your number as the recipient of first-place honors. There is absolutely no reason why you should not beam with pride. Unfortunately, many of us don't realize that we "won" long before stepping into the ring. Equally, you never have to participate in a horse show to be successful. You became a winner the moment you listened to your heart and gathered up the reins of your first mount. The challenge was never the first-place ribbon; the challenge was to acknowledge your desire to ride well and make the commitment to work hard enough to get there. The blue ribbon was the icing on your cake of endless hours of practice and your determination to be a successful rider.

VOICE NUMBER THREE: I CAN'T DO THAT!

Children have little fear and largely what they do possess was learned. Kids gladly take on most any challenge given to them and usually beg to do "it" again. I have shared instructional time with teenagers and have seen this with my own eyes. In lesson after lesson our trainer would point to a series of jumps and tell us our order of go. The children would titter with excitement and say, "Cool, me first!" I would shriek, "YOU'RE KIDDING!" with a tone of disbelief to my voice. That is the fear of being injured speaking. It is also the conscious understanding of a working mother who, regardless of her physical discomfort, must be at her post the next day.

How much pain reliever can a person actually ingest before glowing in the dark? I don't know, but have you ever noticed that children rarely need the contribution of ibuprofen at the end of their lesson? Why is that? It is because children's muscles have not been given years to sit around and do nothing, they have not yet given birth, no "ectomys" have been performed on their bodies, and supplementary medications are not a part of their day-to-day routine. Many of these things are, however, very real concerns for the mature female athlete. As the "chief cook and bottle washer" of most households, it is quite devastating to all concerned when mom gets hurt or sick.

There are other quiet fears that prey on your mind, and therefore, affect your performance. The fear, or concern, that everyone is watching is right at the top of the list. It is true, everyone is watching, but the audience is rarely being judgmental. When you ride in an open ring or an indoor arena, an audience of some sort almost always comes with the territory. Riding demands total concentration, and remembering this will help to block out the spectators. Remember too, that just because other people are there, it does not mean they are actually paying any particular attention to you.

The fear of making mistakes is also a concern. Yes, you will make mistakes, and anyone who says she hasn't is lying! Making mistakes is how you learn. That is why you have a trainer. It is his or her job to teach you and help you correct your mistakes. Therefore, choosing someone with whom you are compatible is very important. All too often, riders find themselves at the wrong barn, so to speak. They and their trainer have serious communication problems, and that is never good for anyone involved. Shopping around for a barn and a trainer can help alleviate that problem before it begins. If you do not have any weak areas in your riding, then you have nothing to work on. It is also simply not true everyone has an area of weakness. Realizing that we all need practice and even the best riders work every day to improve themselves is comforting.

VOICE NUMBER FOUR: SWEAT EQUITY

Simply defined, sweat is a result of hard work, and equity is the value of someone's personal property. In sports, sweat equity is the amount of hard work put forth to realize one's personal best. A rider's level of proficiency will reflect the amount of effort she was willing to expend.

This wonderful sport is very hard work. Only the mechanical horse outside your local discount store requires nothing more than a quarter, and just that much effort, to ride. Remind yourself frequently of all of the calories you are burning along with the immense quantity of sweat. That has always served me well in my quest for inspiration to continue. Mentally add the fact that this day of intense exercise, sweat (not unlike being in a sauna), and the cleanest pores in town was free of charge, unlike a similar day at the spa.

The sweat equity in riding is not only physical, but emotional as well. I can have one of the worst days at school and, once on board my horse, the pent-up tension flows out of my body through the toes of my boots. It is an incredible emotional release. There is also the underlying notion that no one can get you there (at the barn). It is a part of your day that you have allocated for yourself. You have to make the effort, however; the horse and the barn will not come to you. It is far too easy to make excuses for not participating. It's too cold, it's too hot, you don't feel well, and you have too many other things to do, are just a few of the daily excuses we give ourselves to cop-out. The time required to achieve a level of proficiency is not accomplished in a few days. It is accumulated over years of dedication to yourself and your sport. In the end, your reward is a job well done, and that truly should be good enough. Plus, you have had an incredible amount of fun and made some lifelong friends along the way.

VOICE NUMBER FIVE: BALANCE

When you ride, you will eat dirt if you lose your balance and that's a fact, Jack! Knowing this, you work very hard to find your center and learn to move with the horse. When you first start riding, your trainer will not ask you to do something that requires a great deal of skill, so relax. You will work at the walk and perhaps the trot for a long time. Before you know it, you will begin moving your body along with the rhythm of the horse. Balance in the saddle is a skill not unlike finding your balance on a bicycle or a pair of skates. All of these areas take time and patience.

Maintaining your mental balance is then again another issue. There are at least two thousand things that pop up in a day to mess with your mind. In one ear and out the other should be your rule of thumb when dealing with the things you cannot change or correct.

For example:

"Mom, why do the neighbors have better stuff than we do?" questions your child.

Using your years of Mom training, you reply, "Because they do!"

What others possess, tangible or intangible, is something you have absolutely no control over and need to give zero attention to. Someone will always have better stuff and there will always be someone who is a better rider. You are in no way a failure and should never see yourself as such. You are simply in a different place.

However:

"Remember," you remind your family, "this afternoon, I am going to the barn."

"Yuck," one child replies, "that means we will have some casserole thing for dinner."

"Look at it this way," you quip, "the casserole thing, as you call it, will make you appreciate the non-barn days and me, all the more."

These are things you can work with. Your family will survive the "casserole" days and actually be better for it. Perhaps they will learn to do some things for themselves. Remind your family occasionally that you are not a paid employee of the household. As women we have the "everyone needs me" syndrome. You must work very hard not to allow "needs me" to become "everyone takes advantage of me." It is very hard — believe me I understand far too well— but it can be done. Let's not forget, you are a person too.

VOICE NUMBER SIX: PARDON ME, BUT YOUR PANTS ARE RINGING

Where can you go in today's world that there are no cell phones? You probably answered, "Nowhere!" and that is my point exactly. What possible reason could anyone have to use the phone while jumping over a four-foot oxer and yet there it is clipped to her belt? If you did answer the ringing nuisance, the voice on the other end would probably ask the whereabouts of her favorite jeans, what's for dinner or something equally as earth shattering. One of my children once posed the question, "Well, what if I died?" I could not let the opportunity go by responding, "Dead people rarely use the telephone!" So, which is it, are we making ourselves available to respond to a true emergency or simply just making ourselves available?

I am no different from anyone else, and I too own a cell phone. However, I do refuse to take it with me into the barn. You have earned some peace and quiet and the world can wait several hours to talk to you. This is another one of those things over which you have control, but we, as women don't always take the initiative. It goes back to that "everyone needs me and what if" scenario. It is the fear of someone being upset with you or your having caused a problem. In reality, they are upset at their inability to locate their "stuff" and are angry with you for not being available to help them out.

How many times have you been questioned the second you walked through the door, as to why you did not answer your cell phone? Rather than stating the obvious, women proceed with a never-ending explanation, followed by an apology. The truth is you don't owe anyone an explanation or an apology as to why you gave yourself a few hours of uninterrupted time. You are not being selfish to others; you're being considerate of your own needs. For women, learning how to overcome the fear of someone being angry with us takes a great deal of work. I put myself at the front of that line. I can honestly say, however, that I am working very hard to overcome my insecurities in that area.

TIME MANAGEMENT

"There just are not enough hours in the day," is something we have all said at least a thousand times. The reason for coming up short, time wise, at the end of the day is because we did not make good use of the time we had. Oh sure, we did tons of work, but was it done efficiently and effectively? Did we address the most important tasks first? Where did need and want fall on our list of things to do?

I stand before you guilty as charged in the occasional day-to-day misallocation of time spent. I have fiddled around with something totally unimportant only to find myself running behind or simply out of time. In most cases it was due to a lack of organization and good scheduling. Scheduling in your day is very important. I am not suggesting that you create a time line for each day and pledge never to waiver. But I am suggesting that you consider allocating particular days when basic "chores" are addressed.

If you work outside the home as I do, then you are all too familiar with what I call "fractured time," which is, particles of time. For example, in the morning before leaving for work, I remove last night's clothes from the dryer, transfer the finished load in the washer to the dryer, and start a new load. I put dinner in the crockpot, clean up from breakfast, and pack my lunch while listening to the news and the sounds of modern technology agitating my family's clothing. Daisy, my golden retriever, keeps me company during my 30 minutes of morning yoga exercises and getting myself ready for school. As I walk out the door, my wonderful canine companion gets a dog biscuit, a kiss on the nose, and the assurance that I will return.

This is what I define as fractured time. Working mothers rarely have long periods of uninterrupted time. Therefore, maximum use of available time is our ticket to success and sanity.

Getting yourself, your home, and your workplace organized and trying to keep them that way is of the utmost importance. *Webster* defines clutter as "a number of things scattered or left in disorder, litter, or confusion." In most all self-help books or videos, the author or instructor will insist that you rid your life of this chaos. I suggest you check out the works of these professionals for any additional help you may need.

Have you ever walked into someone's office and been welcomed by a voice hidden behind stacks of papers, files, and books? Was it also necessary for you to remove things from the chair before sitting down? This unorganized way of living and working is causing you unnecessary stress. How many times have you spent perhaps hours searching for a particular bill, telephone number, or even your car keys? A place for everything and everything in its place really does work. This allows you time for more important things. No longer are you wasting endless hours on a self-induced treasure hunt rummaging through stacks of junk. I don't know of any home free from stacks, mine included, but they should be organized stacks.

The other form of disarray in our lives is what we, as women, allow other people to pile on our plate. Why are you picking up your children's toys? Why are you making up their beds? Why are you gathering their dirty clothes? Is there someone at your home doing that for you? I doubt it very much. In no way am I suggesting that you turn your back on your family and their needs, but shoveling up behind your children is not taking care of their needs. They need to learn responsibility, cooperation, and group living skills. Those are their real needs. Are you running a home or a hotel chain? This type of clutter leaves you feeling unappreciated, subservient, and exhausted! You have also done this to yourself, and you are the only person who can correct your mistake.

Some of you may think that the age of your children excludes them from helping out, and you are wrong. Even small children can take some responsibility for their things and their space. Do your children have any trouble spreading their toys all over the floor? I didn't think so. Truly, if they can take the toys out, they can put them back. Little children love to be given jobs. It makes them feel important and worthwhile. For example, when you are unpacking groceries, let your child carry the boxes of tissues or toilet paper to the bathroom. Give him or her a dust rag and a particular table that is his or her responsibility to keep clean.

Emptying the clothes dryer was always one of my children's favorite jobs. Each of my girls loved the smell of the clean clothes and the warmth to their hands. They were also just the right size to reach the handle of the dryer, which was a big self-esteem "I can do it myself" builder. Removing clothes from the dryer is a safe activity because that appliance switches off as soon as you open the door. Naturally, you must give careful attention to the jobs you allow your children to do and not to do. Safety is always the number one issue and concern in allowing children to help with certain things around the house.

Again, I am speaking to you as a mom who has been there, done that, and bought the T-shirt! Trust me, I know how hard it is to stay organized, especially with children, but it can be done. There will always be days when nothing works out. Your day was messed up from the get-go. On these days you need to just relax, inhale, and pledge to try again tomorrow. It is the big picture of your life I am talking about. You can't do it all. You can't be everything to everyone. You can't be in more than one place at a time. So why are you killing yourself trying? Get organized and straighten up the clutter in your life. I guarantee you'll have better days.

Celebrate a day of great riding with good food and good friends.
Back Row: Harriet Gayle, Jane Slaughter, Gillian Overing, Susan
Weinbaum. Front Row: Sandra Kabler, Sally Thompson.

DIET

You Are What You Eat

You are what you eat and not just because your mother said so. She was, however, correct. Understanding that potato chips, cookies, and dip are not an actual food group can be quite unsettling. Realizing what is involved in reversing the effects of years of inactivity, an unbalanced diet, and overindulgence in your eating can take you near the edge. However, you and your family will reap the benefits of your new outlook on life and your general good health.

My mother, the nutritionist, has always said that the best diet is, "Some of everything and not too much of anything." I am sure you remember being told as a child to eat your green beans so you would grow tall and strong. How many times were you reminded that lettuce was roughage? To this day, I tell my children that they need to eat their roughage. Naturally, their eyes roll and their lips curl at my advice, and I am holding on to the day I become a grandmother. It will be sweet revenge to see my daughters counseling their children on the benefits of good nutrition.

So what should you eat? How much is too much? Should your food be natural (what exactly is unnatural food anyway) or organically grown? There are thousands of studies out there for your reading pleasure. Hundreds of books line the shelves on the topic of healthy eating. Certified and highly qualified experts in the world of nutrition have spent decades on this subject. I would advise that you check out their writings if you have any medical or physical problems that would require a more individual diet plan. Your family physician can also be of assistance in answering your questions.

In the realm of riding, your being very hungry or dehydrated can be extremely dangerous. You will exert a great deal of energy during a lesson and your body needs the fuel to keep up with your demands. For any given day this is what I would suggest.

- Eat breakfast! Breakfast is the most important meal of the day, it really is. Most of us are working adults and do not have the time to prepare a gourmet morning meal, but we do have time to eat healthy breakfast foods.

- Allow yourself a nutritious midmorning snack such as a piece of fruit or a granola bar. This good-for-you snack will give your body an energy boost while not adding unwanted calories or fat to your system. It will also help you avoid stuffing yourself at lunch.

- If at all possible, walk to and from lunch. Very probably, you have been sittting for most of the morning, and your heart will thank you for taking it out for a walk. Try to stay away from foods drowning in saturated fats. I know, they taste wonderful, but they are killing you. Equally, a meal that provides nothing substantial to your body's needs is a waste of time and money.

- A healthy afternoon snack will carry you into your evening meal. It is a long time between lunch and dinner, and a snack can be quite beneficial. Not only will this afternoon treat energize you for your riding lesson, it may keep you from overeating at dinnertime. Additionally, being hungry interrupts your ability to concentrate and focus during your instructional time. Food for the brain is a very real thing.

- Remember, what you eat at dinner is also going to bed with you. Eating too much or too late can cause you to have a restless night's sleep. The "bad guys" of your evening meal are also not being burned off while you sleep and, therefore, are turning to fat.

- Lastly, drink lots of water during the day. Water is so good for you. It flushes out the toxins in your system, it has no calories, and is very good for your skin. Other sports drinks are OK, but they do contain additives that you may not want. I suggest you read the label before making a selection and purchase. Plus, I cannot allow the opportunity to go by without mentioning that water is free. You can refill your recyclable drinking bottle from the tap. Keeping several bottles of water in the refrigerator at the stable where you ride is a great idea. This allows "do I have everything?" to fall into the category of "one less thing I have to remember." Don't forget to write your name on a piece of tape and attach it to your bottles. This will help avoid any confusion of ownership. Run your water bottles and caps through the dishwasher to keep them clean and sterilized.

Good sense and moderation are the best rules of thumb regarding nutrition. Enjoy your food. Take the time to relax and slow down while eating. Dinnertime is a special time of the day and one that can be a wonderful family gathering. It truly is quality time. So... *bon apetite!*

RECIPES

There will be many days in your riding career in which you find yourself short on time and long on guests to entertain. Preparing a fabulous meal for your friends after a great hunt or horse show does not have to be stressful or expensive. All you need for instant success are organization and some wonderful recipes. As luck would have it, I just happen to have a few incredibly delicious, quick-to-fix, and very affordable suggestions.

If children are on the guest list, be nice, order pizza for them. Children are not likely to enjoy most adult menus, but offer them the choice between what the adults are having and pizza. All too often, we as adults assume to know what children want, but forget to actually ask them. Also, children do not enjoy hanging around the dinner table for hours, either. They would much rather be in the den or playroom watching television or engaged in some thought-provoking video game. So let them! When it is delivered, hand the children the boxes of pizza, a stack of paper plates, and a handful of paper napkins. Your overall goal should be for everyone to have a good time, enjoy a fabulous meal, and be in the company of friends, regardless of their age.

MENU

Scalloped Potatoes
Seasoned Tomatoes
Beef Tenderloin & Dressing
Strawberry Shortcake

Scalloped Potatoes

Jane Slaughter

1. 4 large baking potatoes
2. 1 medium sweet onion (cut in thin slices, then quartered)
3. 2 cloves garlic minced
4. 1 cup milk
5. 1 cup heavy cream (I use skim milk and Half & Half)
6. Salt and ground pepper
7. Just enough flour to sprinkle

Slice potatoes (you can peel the potatoes or not, the potato peel is very good for you) and place in a large pot to boil. Cook the potatoes until they are slightly tender. This will cut your baking time in half and keep the potatoes from becoming dry. Sprinkle the minced garlic on the bottom of a buttered (or cooking spray) 2 qt. baking dish add a dusting of flour also. Using half of the slightly cooked potato slices, arrange in rows. Next, layer half of the onions, sprinkle with salt and pepper and a light dusting of flour. Repeat this process to make the second layer. All of this can be done the day before and stored (covered) in the refrigerator overnight. Save the milk and cream until baking time. Preheat oven to 350 degrees. Pour both milk and cream over the top of the entire dish, trying to moisten all of the potatoes. Bake covered for 30 minutes, remove cover, and tip the dish from side to side to baste the potatoes; cook for 15 additional minutes. This will allow the tops of the potatoes to brown. Let stand for 10 minutes before serving. Serves 10.

Seasoned Tomatoes

Sally Thompson

Slice 6 medium tomatoes; place in dish so tomatoes lie flat. Blend all of the following ingredients and pour over the tomatoes; refrigerate (covered) overnight:

Dressing for Tomatoes
1. 1 large clove garlic (minced or mashed)
2. ½ teaspoon crushed basil
3. ¼ teaspoon each crushed oregano, rosemary, thyme (all fresh)
4. ¼ teaspoon salt
5. ½ teaspoon pepper
6. 4 tablespoons oil
7. 4 to 5 tablespoons vinegar
8. Cut fresh parsley over all at the last minute before serving

Stuffed Beef Tenderloin

Sally Thompson

I know you are thinking that beef tenderloin is expensive and it is, but it isn't. When you consider how many people you can feed from one tenderloin, it becomes quite affordable.
1. 4-5 lb. beef tenderloin roast

Dressing
Sauté all of the following ingredients in 3 tablespoons of butter and salt to taste. Then mix in the cooked rice.
1. ½ lb. mushrooms (sliced)
2. ½ clove garlic (chopped fine)
3. ½ small onion (chopped fine)
4. ½ green pepper (chopped fine)
5. salt, pepper, and paprika
6. 3 tablespoons of cooked rice

Cut slit in roast down the side, fill with stuffing, and tie together with string. Place in bottom of broiler pan and pour 2 tablespoons melted shortening over roast. Pour 1 cup dry white wine and 1 cup of water in the pan, NOT over the meat. Drape strips of bacon over the roast from one end to the other. Cook in 375-degree oven for no more than one hour, basting every 20 minutes. This is delicious served at room temperature. Prepare the meat the day before, cover and refrigerate, cook it in the morning before you leave home, and serve it for dinner. Serves 6-10 people.

Strawberry Shortcake
Jane Slaughter

This is the easiest dessert in the world, tastes fabulous, and takes no time to prepare. Substitute any fruit you prefer or add an additional fruit, such as blueberries, that is in season. Except for putting it all together on a plate, all preparation for this dessert can be done the day before.

1 pound cake (I buy mine in the frozen food section of the grocery store), enough for each person to have one ½-inch-thick slice.

Whipped cream Pour whipping cream and just enough sugar to make it slightly sweet into a bowl. Using a hand mixer, beat on high speed long enough to form peaks, cover, and refrigerate (let your children lick the beaters; it's fun, makes great memories and is good for them. Remember to turn off the hand mixer first, just kidding!)

Fruit of choice sliced if necessary. Large strawberries should be sliced in half, sprinkle with a dusting of sugar, and store in a covered bowl. Place one slice of pound cake on the dessert plate. Add one healthy spoonfull of fruit and top off with a dollop of whipped cream. NO licking of your fingers or spoon until the last dessert is finished.

MENU
Fresh Green Salad
Wild Rice
Basil Chicken
Coconut Pie

Fresh Green Salad
Sally Thompson

Please use a variety of fresh greens in your salad as opposed to a head of lettuce. The fresh greens are easily acquired at most any grocery store; they are healthier, and make for a much more visually appealing addition to your menu, not to mention they taste better as well. Add to your salad a wonderful homemade dressing and your guests will ask for your recipe.

Salad Dressing

1. 6 tablespoons oil
2. 2 tablespoons apple vinegar
3. 1 teaspoon salt
4. 1 teaspoon pepper
5. 1 tablespoon sugar/honey (I use sugar)
6. 2 tablespoons cold water
7. Put all of these ingredients in a glass jar, add a quartered or chopped onion, shake, and let marinate.

Wild Rice
Jane Slaughter

Use your own judgment on selecting the rice. Most boxed or bag varieties of wild rice are quite good. The packaging will tell you how many people can be served from one box or bag. Rice can be made ahead of time. After boiling, allow the rice to cool a bit before storing in a large freezer-weight plastic bag. Keep the rice refrigerated until time to use. Place the bag of rice in the microwave (I open the bag just a bit) and heat. The amount of rice you are serving will determine your heating time. Remove the bag from the microwave and allow to sit for a minute or two before pouring into a serving dish.

Basil Chicken
Gillian Overing

Using a large Dutch oven, pour in 4 cans of chicken broth and lots of fresh basil, bring chicken stock and basil to a rolling boil, and add chicken. Turn boil down and continue to cook for 3 minutes. Leave chicken in Dutch oven with all of the broth and basil, refrigerate for 24 hours. The chicken may be slightly discolored, but don't worry, it's fine.

Sauce

The sauce should be more thin than thick, so add more lemon juice or the liquid from the caper jar to thin the sauce out even more.
1. 1 cup of sour cream
2. 2 tablespoons mayonnaise
3. 1 tablespoon capers (chopped)
4. 1 clove garlic crushed
5. 2 lemons
6. Chopped basil—about a tablespoon
7. Mix all ingredients together and spoon over chicken in serving platter.

Coconut Pie
Cornelia Rankin
1. 3 eggs
2. 1-1/3 cups sugar
3. 7 tablespoons melted butter
4. Pinch of salt
5. 1 teaspoon vanilla
6. ½ cup canned milk
7. 1 can coconut

Beat eggs, add sugar and remaining ingredients. Pour into unbaked pie shells and bake at 350 degrees for 25 minutes. Makes 2 pies using thin pie shells.

MENU
Congealed Cherry Salad
Mustard Asparagus
Roasted Potatoes, Carrots and Parsnips
Flank Steak with Mustard & Capers Sauce
Meringue Shells with Filling

Congealed Cherry Salad
Cornelia Rankin
1. 1 can red sour pitted cherries
2. 1 3 oz. package cherry Jell-O
3. ½ cup sugar
4. ½ cup pecans, chopped

Drain juice off cherries in small saucepan, heat to boiling. Pour hot liquid over Jell-O; stir to dissolve; set aside to cool. Add sugar to drained cherries, simmer about 4 minutes, and set aside to cool. As Jell-O begins to thicken, add cherry mixture and nuts. Chill. This recipe makes one large mold or eight individual molds.

Mustard Asparagus
Gillian Overing

This recipe is for approximately 12 pieces of asparagus; double the amounts for additional asparagus.

Mustard Sauce
1. ½ fresh lemon squeezed
2. 1 rounded tablespoon Grey Poupon mustard (country Dijon style)
3. Dash of fresh garlic

Place asparagus in microwave-safe dish, cover with water, and sprinkle with salt and pepper. Cook for about 4 minutes. Drain off water and pour mustard sauce over asparagus; return to microwave and cook an additional 1-2 minutes.

Roasted Potatoes, Carrots, and Parsnips
Gillian Overing

In roasting pan, add new potatoes (cut in half, peeled or not), carrots, and parsnips. To this add enough oil to cover the bottom of the pan, and to taste add salt, pepper, garlic, and sprinkle with parsley and any other herbs you choose. Bake in 400-degree oven for about 20 minutes covered; bake an additional 20 minutes uncovered.

Flank Steak with Mustard & Capers Sauce
Sally Thompson

This recipe is for two flank steaks and will feed 8-10 people. In large frying pan add ½ tablespoon of butter and oil (olive or vegetable). Cook steaks for 5 minutes on each side; set aside.

Sauce
1. 6 tablespoons butter
2. 6 tablespoons dry vermouth
3. 2 tablespoons mustard (Grey Poupon country Dijon)
4. ½ teaspoon Worchester sauce
5. 3 tablespoons capers

Lower heat in the same frying pan used to cook steak. Add all of the sauce ingredients, whisking them together. Allow to simmer while you cut the flank steak on the diagonal and place on serving platter. Pour sauce over the sliced meat.

Meringue Shells and Filling
Jane Slaughter

Meringue shells are visually impressive and something out of the ordinary as desserts go. You can fill the shells with most anything you choose from fruit to chocolate pudding, top the filling off with some whipped cream, and bingo, instant success. Never make meringue on a rainy day; it will not set up.

Heat oven to 275 degrees. Makes 8 individual shells.

1. 3 egg whites
2. 1 teaspoon vanilla
3. ¼ teaspoon cream of tartar
4. Dash of salt
5. 1 cup sugar

Separate eggs and let whites stand at room temperature. Add vanilla, cream of tartar, and salt. Beat until frothy; gradually add sugar, a very small amount at a time, beating until very stiff peaks form and sugar is dissolved. Cover cookie sheet with ungreased paper (I use a brown paper grocery bag, cut open and lying flat). Draw eight 3½-inch circles; spread each with about 1/ 3 cup meringue. Shape with spoon to make shells. Bake in a very slow oven for one hour. For crispier meringue, turn off the oven; let dry in oven (door closed) at least 2 hours. When completely dry, meringue shells may be kept covered in a dry airy place for several weeks or may be frozen. If frozen, uncover to thaw and place in oven on very low heat if they feel moist in any way.

Taste test for the book's recipes. From left to right: Susan Weinbaum, Gillian Overing, Jane Slaughter and Sandra Kabler.

EXERCISE

EXERCISES IN THE SADDLE

Riding is different from most other sports in the category of "warm-up" time. Why is that, you might ask? Because, not only is it essential for the rider to engage in some preliminary stretching exercises, but it is of equal importance for the equipment used, that would be your horse, to warm-up as well. Other than game-hunting sports that use dogs, riding is the only other venue whose means of participation, as well as transportation, has a pulse. It is very important for a rider to keep that in mind before, during, and after a ride. This wonderful animal has worked very hard for your enjoyment. The least you can do is give your mount the care and consideration he deserves.

Stretching exercises for the rider can include many different elements. As you work on limbering up while in the saddle, your horse will began to stretch out as well. Both you and your horse should start out slowly. Whoever said, "no pain, no gain" was nuts. That sort of approach is physically detrimental to yourself and your horse. A gradual increase in the difficulty of your workout will result in a lasting overall fitness. Starting out with too much, too fast will only cause unnecessary pain and perhaps injury. It may also leave you with a bad taste for exercise and a "forget that" attitude.

"In-the-saddle" exercises are a wonderful way to develop your confidence, your balance, and your ability to trust your horse. Never attempt any of the following exercises when riding alone. In the opinion of this author, it is never advisable to ride alone at any age, but children especially should never be allowed on a horse or pony without the close supervision of an adult. NEVER ride without wearing an approved safety helmet.

It is also comforting to understand that some things in riding are universal. The following warm-up exercises and "how-to" are the same regardless of where you might train. Most all instructors will have their students, regardless of their ability, participate in the exercises included in this section. There is a certain amount of security in knowing that once learned you can perform the "basics" with most any group of riders. Also understanding that the terminology used in the descriptions of these warm-ups is basically the same no matter where you may ride or, with whom, is reassuring as well.

TOE TOUCHING

Photo by Dr. Richard Weinbaum

While at the walk, for the advanced rider, bring opposite arm to opposite toe trying very hard not to move your leg out of position. Start out slowly so as not to lose you balance while in the saddle. Your horse or pony should continue at the walk as you repeat the exercise several times on both diagonals. If you are a beginner, you will need to have the assistance of an adult, who can hold your mount still while you try this exercise for the first time.

LEANING BACK

Photo by Dr. Richard Weinbaum

This is the ultimate test of your confidence in your horse or pony. For the more advanced rider, keep your feet in the stirrups and slowly lean back while the horse continues to move forward at the walk. It may also be necessary for you to let go of the reins so as not to pull the animal's mouth. Slowly count to five and return to an upright position. For the beginner, have an adult hold your mount at a standing position for the first few times. This will allow you to relax while getting the feel of the exercise.

TWO POINT

Photo by Dr. Richard Weinbaum

It is always best to start out slowly when trying anything new. Allowing your body to adapt to the new position will make for a much better experience. At the walk, drop your heels, keep your seat slightly out of the saddle, but directly above your feet; your upper body is tilted slightly forward. The faster you go (at the trot or at the canter) the more forward you tilt your upper body. This is a wonderful exercise in finding your balance and shifting your body weight into your heels.

SITTING TROT

Photo by Dr. Richard Weinbaum

The sitting trot is often required in Hunter "flat" classes at most any horse show. It is almost always required in an "Equitation" class. It is a test of the rider's balance and ability to move with the horse. The sitting trot, using no stirrups, is an excellent exercise for improving a secure seat. The beginner should initially hold the pommel of the saddle with one hand. As you find your balance and increase your leg strength, holding on will no longer be needed to stay on board. The posting trot without stirrups is difficult, but a wonderful exercise for strengthening your calves and improving your balance. Use your knees, your lower legs, and lift your toes. I know-OUCH! But, it is a great exercise.

LEANING FORWARD

Photo by Dr. Richard Weinbaum

This is a very good stretching exercise and should be done at the beginning of your lesson. You will need to keep your feet in the stirrups and lean forward, stretching with your arms toward the house's ears while pressing down with your heels.

TWISTING

There are two very good twisting exercises that will help to stretch out your torso. With your feet in the stirrups, first try twisting with both arms out at airplane position. Next, hold the back of your saddle (cantle) with your right hand and turn your body to the right at your waist. Bring your left arm around until it points to the back of your horse. Repeat both of these exercises until it is no longer a strain on your body.

Photos by Dr. Richard Weinbaum

STANDING TALL

Photos by Dr. Richard Weinbaum

Standing tall in your stirrups stretches out your legs, ankles, and upper torso. It also helps in finding your balance while on your horse. There are two versions of this exercise, and both are recommended. First, with the horse at the walk, stand tall in the stirrups dropping your heels down. Alternate the heels down exercise with standing on your toes for a very complete workout.

DON'T FORGET TO BREATHE!

Proper breathing is essential! In with the good air and out with the bad, in that order, and with a relaxed and even rhythm will help your overall performance. However, if your breathing is too fast, you can become exhausted, perhaps hyperventilate, and may even run the risk of blacking out or falling off your horse. It is essential to relax and remain calm.

EXERCISE: OUT OF THE SADDLE

Thank goodness for dogs and tennis shoes. I owe a great deal of my over-40 rehab to my golden retriever Daisy, Reebok, and my newfound Jack Russell attitude toward my personal health. After years of a somewhat sedentary lifestyle, motherhood, and several "ectomys," I got a grip on my life and put myself on a sensible diet and exercise program. It is very important to be realistic about what you can do and how long it may take to achieve your goals. The weight and inches you take off will stay off if basic fitness and good eating habits become your new way of life.

At the age of 14 my youngest daughter, Taylor, convinced me that buying a puppy, in January no less, would be a great idea. I know you have already finished, this story and yes, on the first bone-chilling day this adorable puppy became *my* dog.

From our initial strolls of insignificant distance, Daisy and I have evolved into walkers of measured miles who constantly try to better our time. Every night after dinner my dog and I delight in our much-loved trek though the neighborhood. During the summer months, considering we live in the South, we start out during the early morning hours trying to beat the heat of the day. My faithful companion and I return to the pavement after our evening meal for an additional 2 miles at twilight, heat and humidity permitting. My realization was two fold: 1) it was my choice to be-

Daisy

come a couch potato, and 2) it was my choice to fix the years of neglect.

Walking is fabulous exercise, but there are many other things you can do for your body as well. Swimming, jogging, weight training, and aerobics are all excellent ways to get and stay in shape. I strongly suggest that you never do any strenuous exercises alone or in the dark. Not putting yourself in harm's way is simply just using your good sense and being realistic in regard to today's society. When you participate in any form of exercise, always be aware of your pulse rate, your overall feeling of wellness, and your basic ability to perform at a given level. The person who suggests that one more mile will not kill you could be wrong, so listen to yourself and to your body.

Regardless of the exercises you choose, it is essential to replace lost body fluids on a constant basis. Ignoring your body's need for liquid can cause serious health problems. Water has been the sports drink of humankind since the beginning of time and has served us well. There are, however, many different products on the market made for the specific purpose of replacing lost fluids. Read the labels carefully, and find the sports drink that best suits your needs.

With there being such a strong focus today on promoting a physically fit society, there are many gyms and health centers available in most areas. These centers offer a wide variety of body-building equipment and individualized programs. Most of these facilities are adequately stocked with individual trainers and it is their job to develop a program that is right for you. Health clubs and the like do come with some form of annual dues, so make sure you ask in advance about the monetary requirements before signing anything. Occasionally people are taken advantage of by a "get acquainted" special only to find out later that the initial price was only for a limited amount of time and the regular dues are substantially higher. Ask for a printed brochure and to have everything in writing. Most gyms are on the up-and-up, but it just takes one to ruin it for all.

For the person who would prefer to remain at home, there are equally as many workout videos and instructional television channels available for the purposes of self-help. I suggest you not look at the woman showing you how-to because, naturally, she has a perfect body; try to simply concentrate on the task at hand.

You work out every day without realizing just how much exercise you are actually doing. So, by becoming aware of what you do on a daily basis, you can work to increase the amount and perhaps the difficulty of each task. For example, going up and down stairs is like having your own stair stepper at home. Stretch to pick toys up from the floor or use leg squats to retrieve fallen items. Park your car farther away from the entrance to the mall. Load your own groceries in the car and return the cart to the store. Take the stairs instead of the elevator in a secure building. Walk from workstation to workstation to ask a question instead of using the in-house telephone system. Carry a pair of tennis shoes to work and walk to and from lunch. Try not to think of exercise in terms of recapturing your youth, because that is ridiculous and impossible. Think of physical fitness as your effort for a better and healthier "rest of your life."

I also am a strong advocate of the benefits of yoga. This discipline is not only good for the body, but its contribution to your understanding of your inner self is priceless. Riding requires physical balance at all times; yoga develops that much-needed balance from the inside out. I have asked my certified yoga instructor, Roxanne Gilgallon, to add her thoughts in this area.

YOGA

by Roxanne Gilgallon

When Jane asked me to contribute to her book regarding yoga and today's equestrian, I was honored. Personally, yoga has changed my life. It has opened up my general awareness about my body and my surroundings. Sounds, colors, and smells that once passed my senses in earlier days, are suddenly awakened. Spiritually, I am more connected. When I practice, I do experience the mind, body, and spirit connection, which is the root of yoga.

For those not familiar with yoga, it originated from India and has been practiced for well over 5000 years. Through the use of asanas, or poses, the body's senses will be awakened along with a higher sense of self-knowledge. Over time, the body begins to strengthen both internally and externally. Greater flexibility is achieved, and the sense of balance is more centered. All of these would benefit an equestrian.

There are at least three important aspects of yoga from which an equestrian could benefit. The first is strength. Riding is very demanding. In yoga, the body moves and holds poses like pieces of art. The muscles are stretched and become stronger. It is this strength that an equestrian draws upon. As the body becomes stronger, the rider's endurance level increases and the body uses less energy, keeping the equestrian from becoming physically drained during and after a ride.

One pose that stretches the chest and shoulders and strengthens the arms and legs, is the "chair pose." To practice this pose, stand with your feet about hip-distance apart. Inhale deeply and raise your arms over your head, palms facing together. Keeping your back flat with your tailbone toward the floor, exhale and bend your knees. Your body will lean forward slightly.

Photo by John H. Burns

Try to keep your back flat. Hold this pose up to one minute and repeat.

The second aspect of yoga is balance. For the horse to use less energy, it is valuable for the rider to have correct posture and to be balanced and centered on the horse. Since the movement of the horse is forward and backward, side to side, and up and down, the rider must become one with the horse. Yoga teaches the art of balance. The mind must be focused and in the present for both yoga and riding. When the rider and the horse feel and understand each other's movements, less physical energy is expelled.

Photo by John H. Burns

The "tree pose," when practiced, will not only strengthen the equestrian's legs but improve balance. There are many levels to the tree pose. Begin with your feet a few inches apart and your hands by your side. Find a focal point, inhale, and raise your arms over your head. Slowly raise one foot up and rest it on either the ankle, knee, or upper thigh of the leg that is supporting you. Hold this pose for up to a minute and repeat using the other side. In my class, many of us practice this pose with our eyes closed, which requires a deep focus from within.

Since there are so many ways in which yoga would benefit an equestrian, I find the area of spiritual connection to be on the top of the list. The third aspect of yoga I would like to share with you is the practice of meditation.

Horses have been found to truly possess a "free spirit." Have you ever watched a horse play, cry, or get angry? Or have you ever seen the reaction of a horse to a certain rider? The reason is that the horse is extremely in tune, not only to his surroundings, but also to the spirit of the rider.

Equestrians have full and busy lives. Sometimes days pass without a moment for themselves unless they are riding. Meditation allows the equestrian to be still. It gives permission to listen and hear the inner voice or spirit, which tends to get tuned out.

As a Christian, I believe we are all at different levels of spirituality. As you practice yoga and meditation, your mind and soul will seem to reach for a higher connection to whatever spiritual path you are currently on. When an equestrian meditates, her spirit becomes awakened. The bond between the rider and the horse becomes stronger. There is a greater sense of trust on both parts. This connection is seen with every ride. As she rides, it appears that the horse is barely touching the ground with each step. The equestrian, sitting tall with her mind clear and her body filled with peace, works with her horse, easing through each movement. Finally, they "experience" the journey as one.

The "lotus" is one of the asanas that is practiced for meditation. Begin by sitting on the floor. With legs straight out, slowly bend the right leg inward, resting the foot on the crease of the left knee. Slowly bend the left leg and rest it on the crease of the right knee. Sitting tall, extend both arms out, resting the backs of the hands on the knees with thumb and index finger together. Close your eyes and breathe deeply.

Photo by John H. Burns

For many, this position may be too challenging for the legs and knees, so I recommend sitting with legs crossed first and gradually trying the lotus, sitting with one leg resting upon the other. You can use pillows to support your tailbone and knees if needed.

To assist in your meditation journey, candles can be lit and meditation music can be played. Try to practice this in an area without distractions. At first, during your meditation, the mind might tend to wander. Some people try to focus on one word by continually repeating it over and over again. Others just ask for guidance. Start out meditating five minutes a day, increasing your time with each day. Just remember that there is no wrong way in practicing meditation. The hardest part is learning to be still.

So where does an equestrian begin to enhance not only her daily life, but also her honored connections as a "woman equestrian?" Today there is a wide spectrum of yoga being offered. The best thing to do before you begin a program is to research the different instructors and facilities in your area. Once you find a home, start out slowly. Regardless of how often you practice yoga, you will notice small changes physically, emotionally, and spiritually.

As you continue on your path, the greatest change for you, the equestrian, will be with your horse. Two spirits, which were once separated, will now soar together as one.

Peace be with you.

Roxanne Gilgallon is a certified yoga instructor, owner of NaturalLife, a Reiki practitioner, a natural health consultant, and is currently finishing her master's degree in Natural Health.

SECTION FOUR
HOW TO RIDE

An infant must first learn to crawl before she stands to take her first step. This is also the attitude you must adopt when beginning your first riding lessons. Too much, too fast can cause emotional upset, a bad taste for riding, and possibly serious injury. Purchasing the proper equipment for your horse is as important as the things you buy for yourself. Asking for help from experts is also a sign of intelligence on your part. Going to a horse show will only occur after a good many lessons and a great deal of preparation. But, it is important to understand the basics of a "show day" beforehand. In your quest to become an educated rider, you will need the help of a glossary. Ignorance is never bliss in the world of riding and horses.

It is also comforting to understand that the "basics" of riding fall under a universal language umbrella. The walk is the walk and trot is the trot. What happens as your horse moves and what you the rider must do to achieve your goal will be the same regardless of where you ride or compete. Your general instruction will be the same regardless of your instructor or location. This global uniformity allows a rider to participate anywhere knowing that her basic skills are correct.

THE BASIC CONCEPTS

THE DIFFERENT GAITS

A horse has four natural gaits or paces: walk, trot, canter, and gallop. The horse moves his legs one or two at a time depending on the particular gait. For practical reasons, it is necessary for the rider to divide the horse's legs into pairs (bipeds):

Front pair: Left foreleg and right foreleg.

Back pair: Left hind leg and right hind leg.

Right lateral pair: Right foreleg and right hind leg.

Left lateral pair: Left foreleg and left hind leg.

Right diagonal pair: Right foreleg and left hind leg.

Left diagonal pair: Left foreleg and right hind leg.

A **stride** is the distance a horse can cover with all four legs (about 12 feet). The number of beats per stride is different for each gait. The walk, for example, contains four beats, one for each hoof. At the trot, however, you will experience two beats as two legs move together in diagonal pairs.

The Walk

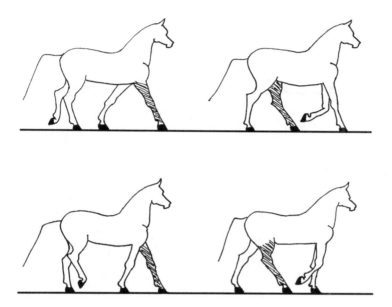

At the walk, a gait composed of four phases, the horse makes four successive beats, moving one leg at a time by diagonals. Each stride is of equal length, and at least two feet are on the ground at the same time. When engaged at the walk, a horse is moving approximately five miles per hour. Looking at the diagrams above you can see the four-beat succession and how the legs move in opposite diagonals.

The Trot

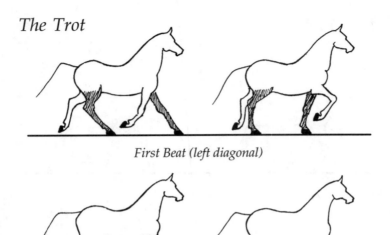

First Beat (left diagonal)

Second Beat (right diagonal)

At the trot, a two-phase gait, the horse makes two successive beats, moving two legs at a time working on the diagonals. Following the diagram above you can see the first beat occurs as the left fore- and right hind leg touch the ground followed by the second beat of the right fore and left hind leg touching the ground. Nine miles per hour is the average speed of a horse at the trot.

The Canter

First Beat (left hind leg)   *Second Beat (left diagonal)*

Third Beat (right leg)   *Suspension Phase*

The canter looks like a mixture of the walk and the trot. At the canter, a four-phase gait, the horse makes three successive beats followed by a suspension phase, when all four feet are off the ground. The horse canters on either the left or the right lead. He is cantering on the left lead when his left lateral pair of legs reaches farther forward than the right. The right lead is when his right lateral pair of legs reaches farther forward than the left. The speed is about 12 miles per hour when a horse is moving at the canter.

Because it is more comfortable, most horses will automatically pick up the correct lead for the direction in which they are traveling. Additionally, horses will adjust their lead, employing either a simple lead change or a flying change of lead, as they change directions.

The diagram above is an example of the right lead. Notice that the right foreleg is the third beat of the canter and the last leg to touch the ground before the suspension phase.

The Gallop

Although the gallop is more a racing gait than a show gait, riders are occasionally asked to gallop during their classes on the flat (walk, trot, canter). The gallop is the horse's fastest pace and is a four-beat gait containing five-phases. Beginning with the left hind leg, it would go like this; left hind, right hind, left fore, and right fore, followed by a suspension phase when all hooves are off the ground. Simply put, there are two beats on each diagonal starting with the hind leg that are followed by a suspension phase. The average top speed at the gallop is about 15 to 20 miles per hour.

DIAGONALS

There are some very interesting words, phrases, and concepts in the world of riding. Most of these concepts are for the good of the horse and the betterment of the rider. It is very important to move with your horse so as not to impede his natural way of going. Remember that the horse is being asked to not only carry all of his weight, but yours as well.

The reason behind posting on one or the other diagonal is to insure that you are rising as the outside front leg diagonal pair is forward and sitting when the inside leg pair is forward. This is helpful when navigating a turn because, during the sitting portion of the post, you can influence and support the horse around the turn. Also, if you always post when the same diagonal pair is coming forward, you may contribute to asymmetrical development of the horse's muscles.

As you go through a riding lesson, your trainer may call out to you that you are posting on the wrong diagonal. Yes, what you are doing is incorrect; yes, you need to fix it, but more importantly, you need to understand what your trainer is saying. Only through understanding comes learning. Look at the drawing that accompanies each explanation.

The Right Diagonal

Your horse is tracking in a counterclockwise direction in the ring. This means you are moving to the left with the railing of the ring on the right. You must post on the right diagonal when tracking to the left. Posting occurs by raising your seat (your bottom) out of the saddle on every other beat. The trick is to post with the correct diagonal leg pairs of the horse. As the right diagonal leg pair moves forward, you should rise out of the saddle. The right foreleg being out in front determines the right diagonal pair. If you miss getting the correct diagonal on the first attempt, sit to one beat and rise again. This should put you on the correct diagonal. When you become a more experienced rider, you should be able to feel the diagonal in your lower leg.

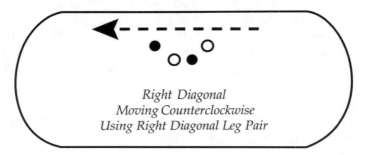

Right Diagonal
Moving Counterclockwise
Using Right Diagonal Leg Pair

The Left Diagonal

Your horse is tracking in a clockwise direction in the ring. This means you are moving to the right with the railing of the ring on your left. You must post on the left diagonal when tracking to the right. Posting occurs by raising your seat (your bottom) out of the saddle on every other beat. The trick is to post with the correct diagonal leg pairs of the horse. As the left diagonal leg pair moves forward, you should rise out of the saddle. The left foreleg being out in front determines the left

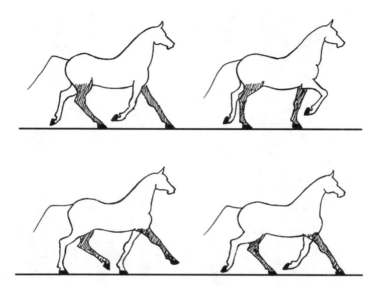

diagonal pair. If you miss getting the correct diagonal on the first attempt, sit to one extra beat and rise again. This should put you on the correct diagonal.

Riding on the Diagonal and Changing Your Diagonal

On the following page is a picture of a class working on the diagonal. The students are tracking in a figure eight pattern. As they each reach the center of the ring, they must switch their diagonal before passing through the ground poles. To do this, you sit for one extra beat in the center of the ring and return to the posting trot. You should find that you are now moving with the opposite, but now correct, diagonal pair of legs. This is a fun exercise to do in a group lesson. The key to this exercise is to relax, breathe, and concentrate on what you are doing.

Photo by Jane Slaughter

Students of Sandy River Equestrian Center practice changing their diagonal while riding on the diagonal.

LEADS

Think of the canter as a combination of the walk and the trot with a suspension phase at the end. Just as you must be on the correct diagonal at the trot, it is very important that you pick up the correct lead at the canter. The leading leg helps to support the horse in the direction he is traveling. In addition, allowing your horse to use the same lead every time can cause uneven muscle development. When your trainer instructs you to canter to the left or to the right, you will need to pick up the correct lead to coincide with that direction.

Using a neck strap on your horse is a good idea when you are first learning to canter. You can hold on to the neck strap for a little extra security while learning to balance yourself. It is also much nicer to the horse than pulling him in the mouth. As you find your balance at the canter, you will notice that you have eased off on the reins and are using your legs more to maintain your balance.

Traveling at the counter-canter means that the outside "diagonal pair" of legs is moving farther forward first and the outside front leg would be the last or third beat before the suspension phase. This is not always an incorrect way of going. Occasionally at a horse show, the judge may direct the riders to show three changes of lead, which would require that you counter-canter. This will only happen at the advanced levels of competition. However, if you are on the wrong lead in the show ring, and it was not asked for, you are very probably out-of-the-ribbons. Whether at a show or in a lesson, it is very important to understand how to pick up the correct lead the first and every time.

Tracking to the right is cantering clockwise, and the right foreleg should move out in front first. The lead legs work in lateral or diagonal pairs with the right lateral pair reaching farther forward than the left.

Teach yourself to focus on what you are doing. It is very important to sit correctly in the saddle and use your legs appropriately. Your seat, your legs, and your hands are referred to as your natural aids and are the ones most often discussed. Don't forget that your eyes, voice, and mind are also very important in communicating with your horse. Your horse has been trained to respond to your commands or your natural aids. The location of your legs, hands, and seat will tell your horse what you want him to do. For example, when you push on an object it moves away from the force of your hand. It is the same with the force of your legs against the body of your horse.

To ask for the right (clockwise) lead, you must sit down in the saddle; if you are too far forward your weight is now over the horse's shoulders. A horse carries 60 percent of his body weight on his forelegs, and now he has you piled on his neck as well. This throws you and the horse off balance. Open your shoulders, relax your lower back, and move your left leg slightly behind the girth. Keeping your right leg at the girth, squeeze strongly with your left leg. By primarily squeezing with your left leg behind the girth, you are telling the horse to step with his left hind leg on the first beat of the right lead canter. You hold your right leg at the girth; only squeezing if necessary to keep him tracking straight. The horse's right foreleg and left hind leg should extend forward first and, way to go, you're on the correct lead! Allow your hands to move with the motion of the horse's head and neck. Do not squeeze with both legs behind the girth, this is the aid asking for the trot.

The canter is a more difficult gait to sit to at first than the walk or the trot. It is more of a rocking motion than an up-and-down motion. The pressure from your legs and the position of the reins in your hands control the speed at which your horse travels. When you first begin to ride and take lessons, your trainer will not ask you to canter. As you find your center of balance and become confident at the trot, your instructor will begin to work with you at the canter.

Take a look at the diagram below and follow the shaded legs for the right (clockwise) lead.

Tracking to the left means that you are traveling in a counterclockwise direction. Just reverse the instructions for the right lead.

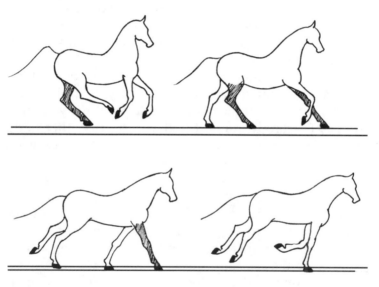

Right Lead: Tracking Clockwise

LEARNING TO JUMP

Jumping correctly requires balance and lots of practice. It is not something you can learn in a day, but children are quicker studies than beginner adults. Can you guess why? If your answer was FEAR, then you are correct. Children will usually agree to try anything at least once. They see any arrangement of poles as a fun way to arrive at the other end of the ring. Novice adult riders, however, being able to factor possible injury into the equation, will often pause for a brief discussion with their trainer before working their way down a line. As an adult, I can report these momentary spells of procrastination to be a total waste of the student's time. Your trainer should never ask you to jump anything that you are not ready to attempt. If your trainer sets up any hurdles larger than a small X-rail for your first efforts, I strongly suggest that you find another barn. NEVER ride a horse without proper adult supervision and ALWAYS wear an approved helmet.

Chin up and look where you are going. There is an old saying that if you look at the ground, you are sure to find it. Looking down also moves your head out of the correct position. Additionally, you cannot properly guide the horse forward if you are not looking where you are going.

Heels down and keep the balls of your feet resting on the stirrup pads. After a while it will become second nature to allow all of your weight to pour into your heels. This is critical in finding and maintaining your balance. It is always important to be balanced when riding, especially when you are jumping. If you are out of balance or in the wrong place on the horse, it will be very difficult for the horse to jump properly. Your weight is in your heels, not on the horse's neck.

Hands forward resting on top of the horse's neck, and grab some mane to help support your upper body.

Keep your eyes up! Your hands should be approximately eight inches in front of the saddle.

Bottoms up and out of the saddle just a bit. You are not a jack-in-the-box, so you should not pop straight up in the air. You will need to lift your bottom out of the saddle and, bending at your hips, lean forward with your torso. This will allow you and your horse to move together in unison over the jumps. Be very careful not to pull on the horse's mouth. He needs the freedom to extend his neck to jump successfully.

Ground poles are a great place to start in learning to jump. They allow you the opportunity to practice your jumping position at the walk and at the trot without actually leaving the ground. Your trainer should always reset a group of poles before each day's work. What was correctly stepped off yesterday has very probably been altered. Incorrect distances between poles will offer you and your horse a bad experience. Remember to relax, put your heels down, and go with the motion of your horse. The distance between the poles for an aver-

Photo by Jane Slaughter

Riders Trotting Poles

Photo by Jane Slaughter

Riders Jumping X-Rails

age horse is four feet. When possible, you should always use three or more poles. Some horses are tempted to jump over two poles. Ground poles can be set at three and a half feet for a shorter stride and up to five feet for an extended trot exercise.

Ground Poles with an X-rail is your next step up the ladder of jumping. The same ground poles you have been practicing over are now finished off with an X-rail (or cross rails). When you are jumping, you must keep your horse moving forward. You do this by using your legs and squeezing to keep him moving toward the fence. Relax, breathe, and stay in the correct jumping position, and you and your horse will sail right over the jump landing safely on the other side. If you are not comfortable initially with jumping, ask your trainer if you may use a neck strap on your horse. This will give you a little extra support and confidence without pulling in the horse's mouth. Again, the distance between the ground poles for trotting is four feet with the cross rail or small jump placed nine and a half feet from the last ground pole.

SAFETY RULES WHEN JUMPING AND RIDING

- ALWAYS wear an ASTM-certified helmet when riding.
- NEVER jump alone.
- NEVER leave the farm by trailer or trail ride without first informing the barn management.
- NEVER leave the jump cups in place without a resting pole in each cup. You may catch your foot or stirrup leather in the protruding cup.
- NEVER allow children to ride without adult supervision.
- Use a ground line when jumping a vertical or oxer jump. It is difficult for the horse to judge the height of an obstacle without a base. Hay bails can be used in place of flower boxes or brush.
- If any horse appears to be ill or injured, NEVER leave the barn until the proper care is administered to the animal.

JUMPING

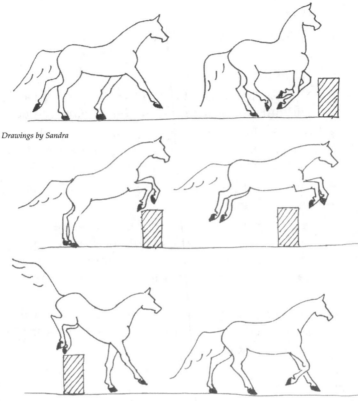

Drawings by Sandra

As a horse approaches any jump, he balances himself and then, using his hind legs, thrusts his body forward and upward. While going over the jump, his legs are tucked tightly under his body, with his head and neck fully extended. The rider must lean forward to allow the horse free movement of his neck and head. When landing, the horse touches first with one foreleg, carefully maintaining his balance, as the other three legs return to the ground.Looking at the horse above, follow his motion and watch as he moves over the obstacle.

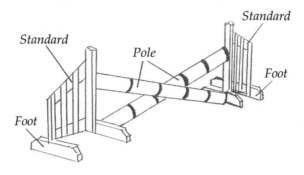

X-Rails or Cross Rails

The beginning rider is usually presented with jumps measuring between 18 inches and two feet in height. Most beginner courses are made up of X-rails (cross rails) or a low vertical pole with a flower box or brush underneath. The course design is also not particularly demanding, allowing the rider the ability to stay focused thus not becoming overwhelmed.

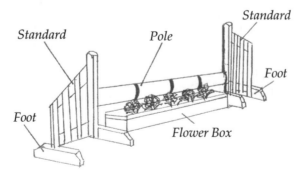

Most jumps are made up of stands (standards), round poles or flat planks, and cups that are also either flat or round. The poles or planks fit into cups, which are secured on the standards by metal pins. A rider may be presented with a solid (in appearance) stone or brick vertical wall. The visual of this towering obstacle can be initially quite intimidating. Understanding, however, that the jump is made of lightweight material and will give way on impact is reassuring.

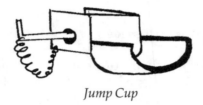

Jump Cup

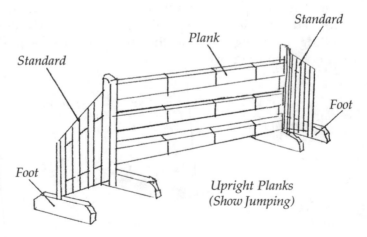

Upright Planks
(Show Jumping)

Jumping a variety of obstacles is always a good idea. Rarely will a rider go to a show and be offered only pole or plank jumps. A jump containing a lead panel will usually have a picture or advertisement of some sort painted on each side. Staring into the painted face of a three-foot fox can sometimes cause a horse to come "unglued." A roll-top jump is also very different from the normal vertical obstacle, because the horse cannot see what is on the other side. Whenever possible, a rider should make every effort to introduce herself and her horse to a variety of jump designs.

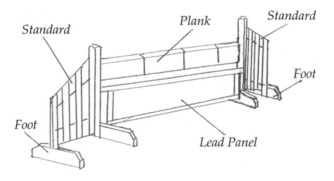

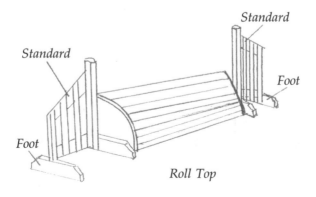

Roll Top

Most pole jumps in a "hunter" course are a combination of colors found in nature. By rule, these jumps should be representative of a hunt field, such as green hedges, birch poles, and natural fences. Jumps in a hunter course should also have a ground line, which allows the horse to judge the height of an obstacle by giving him a base. In a "jumper" course, the poles come in a variety of color combinations, and there is no base or ground line. The standards used are also of different shapes and designs, many of which offer advertising for various sponsors of the event. An oxer is a jump containing two or three separate jumps placed together.

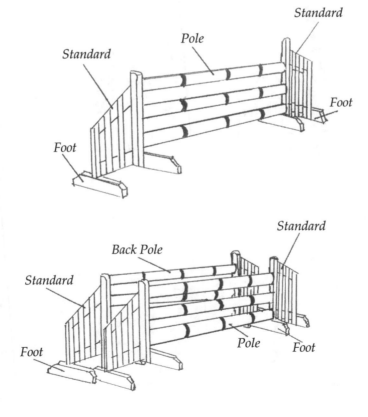

Jumping is an important part of many equestrian sports. Eventing, which includes cross-country jumping, contains very difficult obstacles that are spread out across the countryside. Most cross-country courses are designed to take advantage of the natural terrain; this would include water, ditches, and small drop-offs. Water jumps are among the most difficult. If they only involved the water it would not be so testing; however, these jumps usually contain several stages. For example, the horse may have to jump a pole (usually a large-size tree log), continue downhill, enter the water obstacle, and jump out the other side onto an upward sloping hill. Occasionally, the water obstacle will have a jump in the middle of the water hazard itself. Cross-country jumping is a test of stamina and endurance.

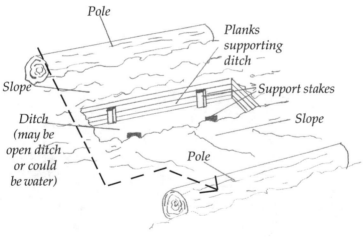

Coffin (Cross Country)

THE SADDLE

History records that at the beginning of the Christian era, the Sarmations were the first to build a saddle containing an interior wooden tree. It would be at least another 300 to 400 years before people rode using stirrups.

Today, saddles are built using an interior tree system as its spine. Trees can be made from wood or synthetics. Pay attention to detail when purchasing a saddle; the better it is crafted the longer it will last. You must also take very good care of this expensive and essential piece of equipment with regular cleaning and proper storage. A saddle should be stored using some version of a saddle rack or stand. This will help the saddle to retain its correct shape and help prevent damage to the tree.

The saddle you choose must fit your horse. Not all horses have "off-the-rack" backs, so you may need the help of an expert in the field before making a purchase. The width of the tree is very important, and not all

Italian Mosaic from St. Mark's in Venice: Jesus on Horseback

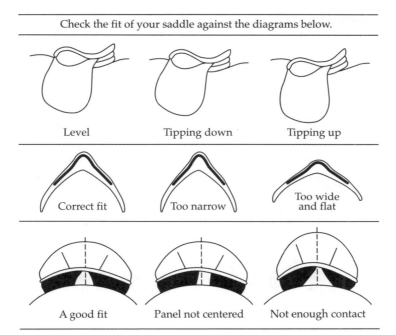

Check the fit of your saddle against the diagrams below.

Level | Tipping down | Tipping up

Correct fit | Too narrow | Too wide and flat

A good fit | Panel not centered | Not enough contact

saddles are the same. The major cause of a sore back in horses is a saddle that does not fit properly.

Take a look at the diagram above and use this as your guide to a properly fitting saddle.

The Parts of the English Saddle

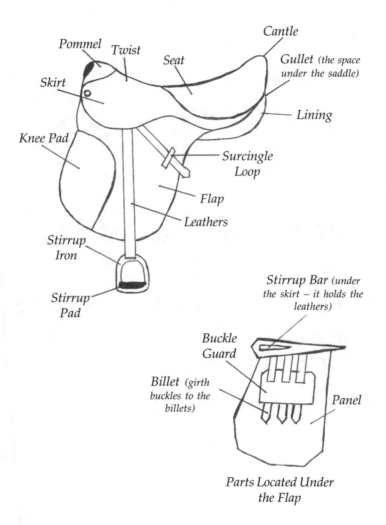

Parts Located Under
the Flap

The Parts of an English Bridle

When purchasing a bridle there are several things to consider. It is a very good idea to ask the help of your trainer or the salesperson at the tack shop when selecting your first bridle. Remember, this particular item of equipment is not for you, but for your horse. Most importantly, it has to fit the horse correctly. Additionally, it must be the correct style for your chosen discipline. Bridles can range in price from around fifty dollars to over five hundred dollars. With this potentially expensive price tag, leave nothing to chance, ask for help.

Different Types of Bits

The earliest known bits were of the thong variety and tied around the lower jaw. The emphasis of the earliest known tack was on control. By 2300 B.C., humankind began to use the bone and horns from other animals to fashion a bit. Metal snaffle bits (containing a center joint) were in common use in the Near East by 1400 B.C. The Celts of Gaul invented the curb bit approximately 1,000 years later.

There are many different bits to choose from, and each bit has a particular purpose. Your trainer can help you in deciding which one is right for your horse. All bits have some type of rings or cheek pieces on either side of the mouthpiece. These rings serve to keep the mouthpiece in place, and are where you attach the cheek straps of the bridle, as well as the reins. Bits can be made from a variety of materials such as metal, rubber, and synthetics. A few of the more common types of bits are shown on the following page.

It is very important to use the correct bit on your horse. Using an incorrect bit can cause a variety of problems. Some of these problems can result in your horse refusing to be bridled, physical damage to the horse's mouth, and creating the wrong carriage of the horse's head.

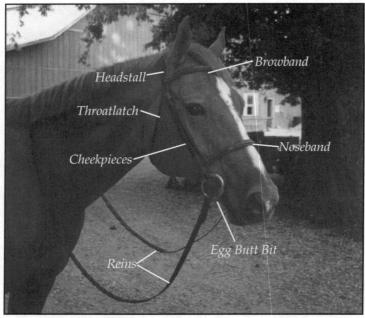

Photo by Jane Slaughter

Dee Ring

A snaffle bit has a
joint in the middle.

Egg Butt Ring

A straight bar bit
has no joint.

Loose Ring

A rubber mouth bit
can be a snaffle or a bar.

SHIPPING HALTERS

NEVER put your horse on any type of transport system (van, trailer, etc.) without first making him "travel ready." It is inexcusable for an animal to be injured due to the owner's lack of attention to detail.

There are several types of shipping halters and each work quite well. I suggest that if you use the fleece-covered leather halter to ship, you also should pack a nylon halter to use while at the show or a visiting barn. The fleece will allow your horse to travel comfortably and lower the risk of rubs and scratches, but it will also soak up every drop of water used to hose him off while away from the barn. What lies beneath the now water-logged fleece is a ruined leather halter. Remember also how hot fleece is in the warmer months. A simple ny-

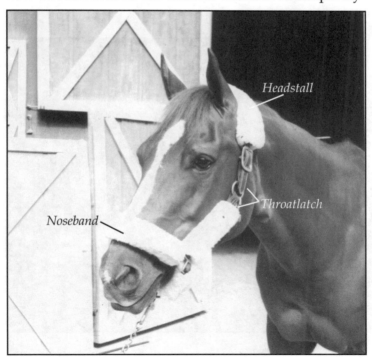

Photo by Jane Slaughter

lon halter with a leather breakaway headstall will be just the thing while at the show. This type halter is also quite adequate for shipping. Make sure that whatever style halter you use, it has a breakaway headstall. This is a safety measure so that the horse can free his head in case of an accident. Leather will tear away, but nylon will not budge. The headstall and the noseband of your horse's halter should have a buckle so as to adjust for a proper fit. You will also need a lead rope, which comes in two basic varieties. The first has a section of chain just after the clip. This chain can be used to thread through the rings of the halter to aid in controlling the horse. The other variety has the nylon cord or leather strapping the full length of the rope. This is your choice and would depend on your personal needs.

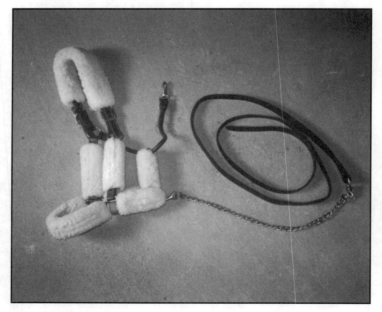

Photo by Jane Slaughter

Fleece-Covered Leather Halter and Chain Lead Rope and Clip

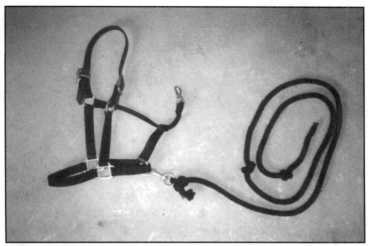

Photo by Jane Slaughter

Nylon Shipping Halter and Leather Breakaway Headstall with Solid Lead Rope and Clip

SHIPPING WRAPS

NEVER put a horse or pony on any sort of transport system without first properly preparing all four of his legs. This can be accomplished in several different ways and is a matter of personal preference. Your trainer will have his or her particular "wrap of choice," and it really does not matter which you use, provided you choose one.

There are two basic solutions to the problem of leg wraps in shipping. One form of preparation is referred to as "cottons and bandages." You will need lots of practice time on chair legs, for example, before actually wrapping your horse. If wrapped incorrectly, your horse can suffer leg injuries from wraps that are too tight. Additionally, these wraps must be placed far enough down the leg so as to cover the coronet band area of the horse's hoof, which leaves the upper portion of the leg unprotected.

The second form of shipping wraps is referred to as "boots." They are much easier to apply and work very well. Make sure when you purchase a set of shipping boots that you have two front boots and two hind boots. These boots are preshaped to fit the contour of the horse's leg and have extra protection for the hoof. They also extend above the horse's hocks adding a buffer between the animal and the back wall of the trailer.

TRANSPORTING A HORSE

Trailering an animal is a potentially dangerous process and must be approached with extreme caution. It is also unsettling for the horse to be traveling down the highway by means other than his own four hooves. With that in mind, extra care must be given when loading and unloading your horse.

When placing your horse on a two-horse trailer, move the middle divider to one side and walk your mount up

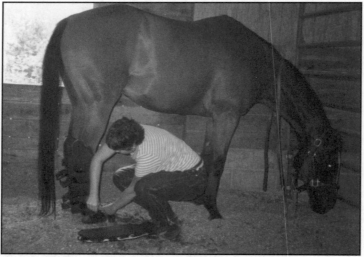

Photo by Pat Wheeler

This horse is an old hand at this; however, it is advisable to tie your horse up while applying shipping wraps or bandages, especially if he has never had them on before.

the middle of the ramp. Take care not to rush this process. If it is a new or different trailer from what your horse is accustomed to, he may be somewhat curious and would therefore need a little time to check things out.

When removing your horse from the trailer, take the time to clean away any droppings. Backing over manure piles on the ramp can cause a horse to slip, which could result in leg injuries or the horse becoming unglued. Again, try and track down the ramp as close to the middle as possible. This allows the horse lots of room on both sides and helps to reduce the chance of injury.

Always sweep and hose out your trailer after every use. Discard any unused hay and open the doors, weather permitting, allowing the entire trailer to air out. You should always have at least a five-gallon container of fresh water on board in the event of an emergency. Other necessary items for your trailer would include a shovel, a muck bucket, a broom, a tire chock, a spare tire, a lug wrench, a roll jack, a flash light, flares, a mini toolbox, a first-aid kit for you and your horse, and a fifth tire rest. It is very important that you are as prepared as possible for almost any emergency.

 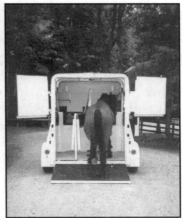

Photos by Pat Wheeler

GOING TO A SHOW

THE SHOW DAY

'Twas the morning of the horse show and all through the barn,
Not a creature was stirring anywhere on the farm;
The buckets were hung by the stall doors with care,
In hopes that breakfast soon would be there.
The barn cats were nestled all snug in the hay,
While sleeping, they dreamed of mouse-filled days;
And I in my flannels and dad less adorned,
Were so peacefully sleeping on a cold winter's morn,
When down at the barn there arose such a clatter,
I hopped from my bed to see what was the matter,
Away to the window I flew double-time,
Threw open the curtains and pulled up the blinds.
The sunrise on acres of wet grass all aglow,
Gave the twinkle of fireflies to objects below,
When, what to my gazing eyes should appear,
But eight SUVs packed tightly with gear,
With eight sleepy moms, none lively or quick,
I knew in a moment they had all been tricked.
More rapid than eagles the riders they came,
And the trainer whistled, and shouted, and called them by name:
"Now, Callie! Now, Katie! Now, Cory and "Z"!

On, Sally! On Gillian! On, Sandra and Lee!
To the racks of the tack room! To the nearest wash stall!
Now wash away! Brush away! Wrap away all!"
As dry leaves that before a thunderstorm fly,
Their pace was equal to a bird in the sky,
So up to the ramp the hay bags they flew,
With a van full of horses, and a Corgie too.
And then, in a twinkling, I heard from the door,
"Go put that back, we can't take any more!"
As I moved from the window, and was turning around,
Down the lane drove the van and headed to town.
They were all dressed in breeches, and tall black boots,
Well-fitting coats, which made them look cute.
A bundle of tack they had flung on their backs,
And they looked like hikers sporting their packs.
Their eyes-how they sparkled! Their smiles so wide,
They were happy to be there, they were ready to ride!
When all was secure it was time to proceed.
"Who wants to school? I'm first! No, it's me!"
Tacked up! Mounted up! Now on to the ring,
The brush box and blankets, the mothers will bring.
First walk, then trot, now canter in line,
"Can we jump the moon?" "No, not this time."
The trainer spoke not a word, but went straight to her work,
And filled all the entries and gave checks to the clerk.
When the day was over, the show a success,
Each rider and horse had all done their best.
As the van was all loaded, each item in place,
A look of relief was on everyone's face.
The trainer sprang to her seat, to her team gave a whistle,
And away they all drove at the rate of a missile,
They were heard to exclaim, as they drove into the night,
"I got all my leads and did each course just right!"

Jane R. Slaughter

GOING TO A SHOW

The Day Before

The day before a show must be devoted to preparation of the rider and her horse. On this day, prior to the natural stress of competition, take care of as many of these chores as possible. Proper organization and a good night's rest are keys to a successful day of riding. Understandably, however, most riders are employed on a full-time basis or are students and are therefore unable to begin this preparation prior to Friday afternoon before a Saturday show. Remembering that time is critical, do everything for the horse FIRST so he will have time to dry before losing the heat of the day. Also, as a "timesaver," consider cleaning the tack (saddle and bridle) after a ride earlier in the week.

The show day is packed with excitement, but also chores, so try to avoid adding any unnecessary stress to an already full plate. Making a prioritized list of "things to do" is a good idea for the novice show rider. In time you will find these tasks a matter of second nature

Equipment: The Tack

Prior to competition, the tack must be properly cleaned, polished, and shined. There are many quality products on the market for the purpose of restoring leather to its naturally supple texture. Be careful not to overdo it using oils. Over time, too much oil can weaken the stitching on saddles and bridles. A good saddle soap or leather cleaner is usually quite sufficient. If using tack that has been neglected for a while, it is a good idea to first wipe the leather with ammonia so as to remove any wax buildup and kill any mold spores that may have developed. Remember to only use a soft cloth or sponge when working with leather items. Using anything else could cause irreversible damage to the surface.

Want the bit and stirrups to shine like new? First soak them in warm, soapy water, then, using an old toothbrush, gently scrub away the grit and grime. The small bristles of the toothbrush will get into those hard-to-reach areas of the bit and down into the tread of the stirrup pads. It is best to use a mild cleanser as opposed to bleach when cleaning the stirrup pads. Bleach can cause the rubber to harden and crumble after a period of repeated use. An electric dishwasher will finish off the cleaning process of the bit and stirrup irons, returning them to their original luster.

Unfortunately, little can be done to erase years of abuse and improper care of one's tack. The best rule of thumb, then, is to properly clean all of the equipment after every ride. This standard isn't practical for most riders, however, so realizing that it is not always possible, take the time to break down the bridle occasionally and give it an extra good "going over." Doing the same for the saddle will keep it in excellent condition for years to come as well. In fact, many people ride using the same tack for decades. Saddles and bridles are very expensive yet are a critical part of the sport. Truly, there is nothing quite so comfortable as a well-worn and properly cared for saddle. For most riders, it doesn't take long for the saddle to become the most treasured piece of equipment, so exercise consistent discipline in its proper care.

The Horse

When entering the show ring, all eyes are on the rider and the horse. If a rider's mount is dirty, improperly groomed, or unkept in any way, her chance for success is virtually over before it began.

Time being of the essence and the heat of the day often even more critical, preparation for a show must begin with the needs of the horse. Pulling the mane is a very time-consuming task, and an earlier day of the week should be allocated for that job. It is a good idea to trim the horse the day before the show if possible. However, a full body or trace clip should be done about a week before the show. It is best to tend to all of the clipping jobs after the bath if possible. Dirty animal hair will ruin a set of clipper blades, which are, unfortunately rather expensive. Also, make certain to shave the bridle path (area just behind the horse's ears), whiskers, ears, and feathers.

There are several schools of thought on the clipping of the ears. Some say that all of the hair inside of the horse's ears should be shaved. Others contend that removing all of the interior ear hair allows free passage for insects and, thus, infection, and that only the hair along the outer edge of the ear should be trimmed. In this area, the rider should take the advice of her trainer. The clipping of their whiskers or bridle path does not trouble most horses. Their ears, however, can be another story all together. Sometimes clipping a horse's ears requires the use of a twitch (an apparatus used to twist the nose of the horse, forcing his attention on his nose, causing him — most of the time — to ignore the clippers) or even tranquilization. Looking at it from the horse's point of view, it must sound as if the world's largest bee has flown into his ear. The vibration of the clippers can also be very disturbing to this sensitive area of his body.

A rider must exercise a great deal of patience and understanding when grooming her horse. Grooming is, after all, a very "unnatural" process. Some horses may actually nip at their rider when being brushed. This may not be an act of aggression, but simply that, just as humans, the horse could be ticklish. A horse will often let his rider know when he has had enough and would like to be left alone for a while. For example, he might start moving away or tossing his head. If possible, take the horse out to graze when finishing the grooming process. Horses usually tolerate being brushed much better when they are otherwise occupied eating grass. Taking the horse out to graze offers a dual advantage: the warm circulating air helps to dry the horse from his bath and the rider can brush until her heart's content.

However, if the weather is cold, the horse should be blanketed after his bath. There are many products available on the market for this purpose, and they are an excellent purchase for the rider who shows throughout the year. Not only do these blankets provide warmth, they also wick away the water on the horse's coat, thus speeding the drying process. One point that many riders overlook: always use clean blankets. During the winter months this can be difficult, but with proper planning, can be achieved with relative ease.

Clipping away the "feathers," the area of long hair at the horse's heels or fetlocks, is also important as it helps keep this area clean and dry. This process isn't terribly complex. Make certain to keep the clippers moving in an upward motion from the ground, being careful not to nick the horse's heel.

The Horse's "Things"

Going to a horse show does not parallel moving away from home. Remember this and try to pack only the things that are needed for the rider and the horse. It is quite possible also that the rider and her horse will not be alone, but traveling with others, so *space* is a definite concern both in the car or truck and the horse trailer.

Necessary horse "things" include an assortment of brushes (each brush really does have its own job), a bucket, several clean rub rags, a hoof pick, fly spray, a sponge, hoof paint, and a blanket or scrim sheet (depending on the weather). There are many different versions of a brush box, the best of which are the plastic variety with two divided sides and a handle in the middle. Plastic is preferred to wood as it is both easier to clean and lighter in weight. And no matter how careful one is, things spill and get spilled upon. Using a plastic brush box helps to prevent equipment from being ruined. The plastic groom boxes also fit securely over fence railings and the stall door, an added advantage considering a rider only has two hands.

Many horses would insist that a bag of carrots be added to the list of "essential" items. Carrots are a better idea for a natural treat, if you so indulge, than apples. The "forbidden fruit" contains a great deal of natural acid that can often upset a horse's stomach as well as sugar that can cause excitement. Horses are already more excited at shows than when at home, so adding extra acids could cause unwanted problems. When taking a bag of carrots, be sure to poke a hole in the bag allowing the moisture to escape. A sealed bag left all day in a hot place becomes a virtual pressure cooker for carrots, quickly rendering them to mush.

The Rider's Things

The rider also has specific needs. Staying clean is perhaps the most difficult problem for competitors, while staying warm follows closely behind. Regardless of a rider's age, this is a dirty sport, but yet the rider is judged on her appearance in the ring. Having a large spot of "who knows what" on the leg of one's breeches is simply unacceptable. If the rider is participating in a two-day show and has only one pair of breeches, cleanliness is of utmost importance. Over the years this author, who is also a mother of a child rider and an exhibitor herself, has learned a few tricks that can help.

If a rider does get something on her breeches and cannot get them laundered before the next day (if staying in a hotel, for instance), wet the soiled area and, using mild hand soap, scrub gently until the spot is removed. Rinse thoroughly, trying not to get any more of the pants wet than necessary. Secure the hanger over the shower rod allowing any excess water to drip into the bathtub. Before going to bed for the night, use the hair dryer on a warm setting to get the drying process well underway. It also helps to place a hand towel inside the breeches and one on the outside. Lay the pants on the floor and press down on them using your foot. This will help absorb some of the moisture and will also put the crease back into the pant leg.

A pair of wind pants is an essential item of clothing for the equestrian. Pants designed with snaps down the sides are the best. If a rider dresses in her show clothes before leaving home, put the wind pants on before stepping outside. These pants will help keep the rider clean all day and can be easily removed just before her division begins. The lined version of these wind pants is fantastic, keeping the rider both clean and warm throughout the winter months.

During the warmer months, wearing a T-shirt or polo shirt until show time is a preferable alternative to wearing a show shirt. Slipping into one's show blouse just before competition is much easier than putting on breeches and tall boots. When the temperatures are colder, most riders choose a coat with snaps or a full-length zipper that will fit loosely over their show coat, as to avoid dragging their coats over their helmeted heads.

The Child's Things

When dressing young children, have them outfitted before the show, add wind pants and an oversized T-shirt, and let them go. Children under 10 years of age show in jodhpurs, garters, and paddock boots. Trying to put all of that on just before their class can be a nightmare! It is truly an endless battle, not just between the adult and the child, but with the surroundings as well. Seldom is there a place free from shavings or hay, and bits and pieces of both always seem to find their way down a child's shoes and/or pants. "Someone might come by and see me" is a constant concern for many girls, rendering them unable to stand still. When it is time for their division, children are hot and sweaty from playing with their friends. Their jodhpurs, therefore, refuse to slide on without a fight, and parents spend what seems to be forever trying to remember which way the garters start and are almost always wrong having to begin again.

For those with a daughter, her hair is the last thing to repair. Before leaving home, her French braids would have no doubt impressed the likes of a master stylist. Yet, as the day progresses, these once perfect braids have now taken on the whimsical look of the scarecrow in *The Wizard of Oz*. This "repair job" is done on the run with a fidgeting little girl who just wants to hop on her pony and ride. She couldn't care less if her braids are straight or if the blue ribbons lose their mooring during her class.

Overall, the best thing for a mother and child is to get as many of these tasks done as possible while still at home in the quiet, early morning hours. Once on the show grounds, most children do not want anyone to know they even have a mother, much less suffer through her fussing all over them, that is of course, until they need money.

Find yourself unprepared with a crisp wind and a cold child? Purchase a sweatshirt from one of the vendors on the show grounds. Be certain to turn the sweatshirt wrong side out before putting it on her. This will prevent her show coat from being covered in lint. The sweatshirt should be extra large so it easily slips off and on over her helmet and show coat.

Regardless of the age of the exhibitor, an approved safety helmet is required. Fortunately, safety is at the forefront of this sport. Occasionally, accidents happen and people are injured no matter how much attention

Photo by Jane Slaughter

Lydia Whitley chats with onsite vendor Lynn Thompson, owner of Horse and Rider Tack Shop in Greensboro, North Carolina.

is given to personal safety. But a rider can NEVER take safety too seriously! A good trainer will advise her riders along the way, offering instruction on safety issues.

Manners

Bad manners, regardless of the circumstance, are never acceptable. The way in which a rider presents herself is oftentimes the lasting impression, even if it is misunderstood. Rarely does a rider have a second chance to make a good first impression.

Exercise some self-control when at the barn preparing for competition. Most riding facilities have one, perhaps two, wash stalls, yet everyone wants her turn first. Wherever a rider may fall in the rotation of turns, she must maintain a diligent work ethic so the remaining riders have ample time to wash their horses as well. She must always remember to clean up behind herself and her horse. If she leaves her cleaning supplies and equipment in the wash area, she is inviting others to help themselves. She should organize all of her things in a plastic tote of some sort. This will make travel to and from the wash stall a much simpler process. It will also help to avoid the unwelcomed question, "Who used my stuff?"

Preparing for a horse show is fun and exciting, but can also be very stressful. Keeping this in mind will help to alleviate any hurt feelings, especially with children. Conflicts are often based on the fact that riders participate on different levels including riding experience, age, and logged show miles. The veteran "horse show" child will quite often, though unintentionally, forget the less experienced riders could use some help. Indeed, an experienced rider can help in ways one can only begin to imagine. It is difficult, however, for some older riders to remain patient with younger or inexperienced riders. The advanced equestrian should give herself a quick trip down memory lane. A "May I make a friendly suggestion?" attitude is almost always welcomed and appreciated by the recipient. Conversely, the "I know more than you ever will" approach is rude, hurtful, and quickly rejected. Try desperately NOT to present yourself as a know-it-all. Even valuable words of inspiration will fall upon deaf ears. Your mother was right when she said, "It's not what you say, but how you say it."

While at the horse show, be polite, punctual, and patient! Horse shows NEVER begin on time nor do they run according to schedule. It isn't because management doesn't want to be timely; it is simply the nature of the beast. For instance, a barn may have only one trainer who needs to be in ten places all at once. Everyone involved in showing understands that this will be a long day, but some things can be avoided to save time. For instance, riders should be schooled (warm-up time prior to the beginning of the show day or before a division) and at the in-gate on time. A rider should pay attention to the clock and have herself ready without having to be told. Ask for help if it's needed, but don't become dependent on someone else. It never killed anyone to say please and thank you, and hearing those words is always appreciated. If it is necessary for a rider to leave a show early, for whatever reason, make sure this issue has been discussed in advance (if at all possible). When it is a spur-of-the-moment situation, a rider must realize that she is leaving the other riders at her barn shorthanded. Try very hard never to leave before the end of the day. Usually, the riders all come together, show together, and should all leave together.

Be a good loser and an even better winner. Everything is just "hunky dory" between friends until one child beats another. Understandably, a rider is thrilled with her first-place honors and the pinning of the blue ribbon. What is not acceptable is for the rider to flaunt her success in the face of others. Statements and questions like, "My horse was Champion today. How did you do?" could cost a rider every show friend she has. Try to be very gracious during the competition day. Once the rider has returned home, jumping up and down, calling all relatives, and hanging the ribbons on the wall is more than acceptable and deserved behavior.

The word "loser" is a relative term, defined in many ways depending upon who is asked. Some unfortunately have the attitude: "Second place is first loser." The true rider should be appalled at such an attitude.

Competition is good for everyone, but only when approached intelligently. Indeed, competitive sports, if fostered correctly, can give children a sense of self-worth, discipline, pride, responsibility, and decision-making skills that will serve them well for a lifetime.

The Dog

It is best to leave the family canine at home when going to a show. These animals really can't be happy locked up in the tack stall. In addition, the exhibitors who keep their equipment in the same tack stall will not be pleased to learn that a dog was not taken on a walk soon enough and has found it necessary to relieve himself on their tall boots. Likewise, being dragged from ring to ring would not offer a "fun day" memory for man's best friend. Being stepped on by horses and people at every turn would not be construed as enjoyable to a pet, either. During the day of a show, exhibitors will hear the announcer reminding everyone that all dogs must be kept on a leash. Shortly thereafter, "If you are missing your dog, he can be picked up at the show office after you pay the fine," will echo over the loud speaker. Sometimes it is simply impossible for one to leave a pet at home, but if the animal must be present, the rider should make every effort to be considerate of her dog and the other exhibitors.

In addition, it would be mortifying to know that one's dog, running through the ring during an over-fences trip has caused the horse on course to spook and ruin a — up until then — perfect round!

The Trip Home

Start with the fact that everyone is exhausted! Each exhibitor has been awake since early morning and has not stopped all day. This fatigue understandably can result in irritability. Remaining organized will help to avoid some unpleasant situations. If a rider has kept up with all of her things during the day and made certain to place them back in their proper place, then her job is better than half done.

As soon as your barn arrives at the show, it is "helter-skelter" to say the least. The trainer tells everyone to hurry up and get the horses ready to school. With that command, shipping wraps become airborne, blankets hit the ground, and grooming tools go everywhere. This process is not nearly as bad as it sounds unless the momentary disorder remains throughout the day.

When a rider returns to her stall area after schooling, she should always take care of her horse first. Once those chores are completed, she should go to work on organizing her things. All of the shipping wraps and bandages must be rerolled if they were used to transport the horse. If shipping boots were used, hose them off and stand them beside the stall to dry during the day. Fold all blankets, towels, and rub rags, and then hang them over the stall door or put them in the tack room. This careful attention to detail allows a rider to enjoy the show day, find her things at any time, and be ready to load her horse for the return trip home.

Remember, the rider goes to the show with a group of people. It is very aggravating for others to always be held up by one person. Work hard NOT to become that person — the one who is chronically late, never knows where anything is, constantly asks for others to help her, and seemingly tries to get out of doing any work by offering a myriad of excuses.

Returning things to the trailer or van throughout the day will also speed up the packing process. For example, when the last horse has had his bath, wrap up the hose and pack away the washing supplies. As the last exhibitor readies for her final division, the finished exhibitors of this group can begin to return all chairs, fans, groom boxes, tack trunks, etc., to their travel spot on the trailer. Most adults who show also have to go to work the next morning; therefore, returning home at a decent hour is highly desirable. Chances are, all of the children who show will be sound asleep in the car or truck before leaving the show grounds, but they will still require a good night's sleep before school on Monday morning.

A Personal Note

I cannot ignore the opportunity to mention this one personal and very important thought. Please work very hard NOT to be the "show Mom" who does everything for everyone's child including your own. In my younger years, I was that person and, using my 20/20 hindsight, it was a very wrong thing for me to do. It was a burden I put upon myself without actually realizing what I was doing until it was too late. It was also a clear disservice to my own child as well.

My daughter, Taylor, began showing at a very young age. She, along with a gaggle of other little girls, went to a horse show nearly every weekend, especially during the summer months. Because I am a teacher and have the summer off, I was the only mother who was able to attend every show, or so I thought. I found myself driving every weekend and tending to all of the children's needs. It never occurred to me that had I refused to ferry these children everywhere, someone else would have stepped up and taken over the driving responsibilities.

I allowed the fledgling exhibitor's lack of organizational skills to drive me crazy. So, instead of teaching them how to be responsible and insisting that the girls get their individual things collected, I did it for them. I allowed them to give me the lead rope attached to their pony and take said pony to graze. Rather, I should have immediately pointed the child and her pony in the direction of the grass, mentioning as they passed by that it was her responsibility.

I was, without question, the most popular horse show Mom of all time. It was only later, however, that I realized why. There is a happy medium to all of this and you need to work very hard to find that place. Helping is one thing, but becoming the "step-and-fetch-it" for everyone at the barn is quite another.

HORSE TALK:
A GLOSSARY

Every sport has its own language, but none quite so interesting as the one spoken by "horse people." When someone offers you a "leg," he or she is not talking about actually giving you an appendage nor is the person offering you a turkey drumstick. The individual is asking if you would like some help getting on your horse. Equally, if an observer tells you that you have a lovely seat, he or she is not being fresh. This comment means you sit well with the horse and look natural in the saddle.

I will never forget the first bill I received from my veterinarian. In the list of charges were various inoculations, deworming, floating teeth, and the inevitable farm call charge. Shots and worms I understood, but why in the world would you float your horse's teeth? If they are detachable, humans would float their teeth in a glass at night, but I knew without question that my horse's teeth were firmly rooted in his mouth. Having no glossary with which to refer, I decided to give my veterinarian a call. He was very nice and quickly explained the term. Returning the receiver to the base, I remember thinking, "If you don't actually float their teeth, then why do you call it that? Strange!"

Beginning on the next page you will find a collection of some of the most commonly used terms on the subjects of horses and horsemanship. Hopefully, this glossary will help you in understanding instructions from your trainer and the terminology used in everyday conversations around the barn and at the showring. If there is ever anything you do not understand, do not hesitate to ask. In the world of horses, ignorance is never bliss.

A

AGED: A horse that is seven or more years old.

AIDS: The signals that a rider uses for communicating with a horse; for example, the hands, legs and voice.

ARENA: An enclosed or covered area for training, schooling, and showing horses. The surface does not become too hard or too muddy in bad weather.

AMATEUR: One who receives no compensation for his/her activities in the sport.

ASS: A member of the Equidae. The two existing groups of wild asses are the Asian wild ass and the African wild ass.

B

BALK: When a horse is stubborn and refuses to move in the right direction.

BARS: The two areas inside a horse's mouth, one on either side, where there are no teeth. The bit is placed across this area.

BIT: A piece of tack attached to the reins, that fits across the bars in a horse's mouth.

BLINDERS: Leather flaps attached to the bridle, used to prevent a horse from seeing anywhere other than in front.

BODY BRUSH: A soft, shorthaired brush you use for cleaning a horse's coat.

BOMB PROOF: A horse that is not easily frightened, which is ideal for beginners.

BREAKING: The initial training of a horse for riding or harness work.

BRIDLE: A piece of tack that goes on the horse's head for riding. It is made up of the headstall, browband, throatlatch, cheek pieces, noseband, reins, and bit.

BROWBAND: The part of the bridle that fits around a horse's forehead.

C

CANNON BONE: A bone in a horse's leg. In the foreleg, the cannon bone is between the knee and the fetlock. In the hind leg, the cannon bone is between the hock and the fetlock.

CANTER: A horse's gait to which the rider sits; similar to a gallop, but slower and more collected.

CANTLE: The upward curving back of the saddle.

CAST: When a horse has lain down in his stall, wedging himself against the wall so that he is unable to get up.

CAVALETTI: Poles 10 feet (3 meters) long that are supported on crossbars for jumping.

CAVESSON NOSEBAND: The simplest type of noseband. A cavesson is also a type of halter that has a ring on the noseband for attaching a lunge line to.

CHESTNUT: The horny, oval pad found on the inner side of the forelegs and on the inner side of the hocks on the hind legs. The term chestnut is also used to describe a reddish gold coat color.

CLEAR ROUND: Jumping each fence in a competition without the horse knocking the rails down, refusing, or running out.

COLIC: A severe stomachache in a horse caused by his having swallowed something indigestible. Horses are unable to vomit.

COLLECTION: When a horse is driven up on the bit, flexing his head and neck, his stride shortened and in perfect cadence.

COLT: An ungelded male horse less than four years old.

CONFORMATION: The overall shape of a horse or pony and the way that it is put together.

CONTACT: When there is no slack in the reins the rider is said to have contact with his horse's mouth.

CORONET: A sensitive area around the top of the hoof where it joins the leg.

COUNTER-CANTER: A horse is said to be traveling at the counter-canter when he is cantering on the left lead, tracking clockwise, or on the right lead, tracking counterclockwise.

CREST: A ridge on the top of the neck.

CRIBBING: A noise made by sucking air down the throat. Usually out of boredom.

CURRYCOMBS: Metal currycombs are used to remove the hairs and oil from a body brush. Plastic and rubber currycombs are used like a dandy brush to remove mud and hair from the horse's cost.

D

DAISY CUTTER: A good mover; a horse who moves close to the ground.

DIAGONALS: Since the trot is a diagonal gait, the horse's right hind and left front legs move together, and the rider must post on one diagonal or the other, coming down in the saddle when either the right or left front foot of the horse is on the ground.

DISMOUNT: To get off a horse.

DOCK: The bony part at the top of a horse's tail.

DONKEY: A member of the Equidae. The donkey is a domesticated ass descended from the African wild ass.

DORSAL STRIPE: A band of black hairs that extends along a horse's back.

DOUBLE BRIDLE: A bridle with two bits in the horse's

mouth (a "curb" and a "bridoon"), used for highly trained horses taking part in dressage and showing classes.

DRESSAGE: A sport in which a horse is trained to perform special movements in a particular way.

E

EGGBUT: A type of joint on a bit that stops the corners of the house's mouth from being pinched between the rings and the mouthpiece of a bit.

ELBOW: The bony point at the back of a horse or pony's forearm.

EQUIDAE: A family of mammals consisting of horses domesticated asses, wild asses, and zebras.

ERGOT: A hard (but not bony) lump that sticks out from the back of the fetlock joint. It is usually hidden under the feathers.

EVENTER: A horse that is trained for show jumping, dressage, and cross-country riding.

EXTENDED: Moving in long strides but in perfect cadence and with great spring and rhythm. At the extended trot the horse's toe hits the ground forward of his nose.

F

FARRIER: A trained person who takes care of a horse's hooves and fits new shoes.

FEATHERS: The long hairs that grow at the back of the fetlock joints.

FETLOCK JOINTS: The joints that stick out above the horse's hooves.

FIGURE EIGHT: A movement that you make in the shape of the number eight.

FILLY: A female horse less than four years old.

FLANKS: The horse's sides, between the ribs and the back legs.

FLEABITTEN GRAY: A white horse with a freckled coat.

FLEHMEN: When a horse curls its top lip in response to an unusual smell or taste.

FLOATING TEETH: The filing down of the sharp points of horses' molars, which prevent them from chewing their food properly and discourage them from eating.

FLYING CHANGE: A change of leads at the canter in air, without stopping.

FOREHAND: The front legs and shoulders of the horse.

FOAL: A newborn horse (up to 12 months)

FORELEG: A horse's front leg.

FORELOCK: The part of the mane that lies between the ears and falls onto the forehead.

FORWARD SEAT: The riding position for jumping or galloping when the stirrups are shortened to help balance. The faster the pace, the shorter the stirrups need to be.

FROG: The v-shaped, horny pad on the bottom of a horse's foot that acts as a shock absorber.

G

GAIT: A horse's pace, such as walking, trotting, and cantering.

GALLOP: The fastest of the horse's gaits; an extended canter.

GELDING: A castrated male pony or horse.

GIRTH: A strap placed around the horse's belly to keep the saddle in position.

GOOD KEEPER: A horse who eats well and is easily kept in good condition without a great deal of care.

GRAZING: The paddock or field where a horse is turned out to graze.

GREEN: A horse without experience or knowledge.

GROOMING: Brushing a horse's coat to keep its skin clean, shiny, and healthy and keep the horse comfortable by removing dirt and dander.

H

HACKAMORE: A type of bridle that cuts off horse's wind.

HALTER: A simple headstall, noseband, and throatlatch for catching, tying up, and leading a horse or pony.

HANDS: A unit of measurement that equals about 4 inches (10 centimeters), used for determining a pony's height.

HAND GALLOP: An extended canter, not as fast as a full gallop.

HAUNCHES: Rump and hind legs of a horse; hindquarters.

HEADSTALL: The part of the bridle or halter that lies behind a horse's ears.

HERD-BOUND: Refusing to leave a group of horses and, once having left them, attempting to return to the herd.

HINDQUARTERS: The back end of a horse or pony including the hind (back) legs.

HOCK: The joint on a horse's hind leg.

HOOF PICK: Usually, a metal instrument curved on the end used to remove mud and debris from the underside of the horse's hoof.

I

INSIDE LEG OR HAND: The rider's leg or hand that is on the inside when he or she is riding in a circle.

J

JUMPS: An arrangement of standards and poles creating an obstacle for jumping.

K

KNOCKDOWN: In open jumping when a horse lowers the height of the obstacle by removing a rail either with the front or hind legs.

L

LAME: When a horse or a pony has an ailment or injury that makes it painful to move normally.

LAMINITIS: Sore hooves (also called "fever in the hooves"). It is usually caused by overtreating.

LEAD LEG: The front leg that reaches farthest forward when a horse is cantering.

LEAD OFF: The moment the horse's pace changes from the trot to the canter.

LEAD RIDER: The rider at the front of a group of riders.

LEFT HAND TO LEFT HAND: When two riders pass each other with their left hands and the horses' left sides facing.

LEG UP: When someone helps a rider spring up onto the horse.

LOADING: Leading a horse or pony into a trailer.

LOOSE RING: A type of snaffle bit, where the bit rings are not fixed to the mouthpiece but can be pulled through it.

LUNGING: When a horse is being trained on a lunge line attached to a cavesson. The trainer stands on the ground and works the horse around in a circle, using a lunge whip to keep the horse going forward.

M

MAIDEN: A horse who has never won a race or a prize.

MANGER: A fixed trough in a stable that a horse can feed from.

MARE: A female horse that is four or more years old.

MASTER: The Master of Foxhounds of a hunt.

MOUNTING BLOCK: A low block of steps for a rider to stand on for mounting.

MULE: The offspring of a male donkey and a female horse.

MUZZLE: A horse's nose, lips, and chin.

N

NEARSIDE: The left side of a horse when you look from the back toward the front.

NECK STRAP: A strap that is placed around the horse's neck for a beginner to hold on to for extra safety.

NOSEBAND: The part of the bridle or halter that lies around the horse's nose.

O

OFFSIDE: The right side of a horse when you are looking from the back of the horse toward the front.

OUCHY: A horse that seems afraid to put his feet down due to lameness.

OUTSIDE LEG OR HAND: The hand or leg that is on the outside when a rider is moving in a circle.

P

PASTERN: The part of the horse's leg between the fetlock and the hoof.

PELLHAM: A type of bit with two reins that works in a similar way to a double bridle.

PICKING OUT A STALL: Removing waste from the stall bedding using a pitchfork. This is very important to aid in the well being of the animal.

PINTO: A horse's coat that is patched with white and any color.

POLL: The part of the head between the ears.

POMMEL: The raised part at the front of a saddle.

PONY: A pony is one that measures 14.2 hands or less. Ponies are divided into three categories: small, medium, and large.

POST: To rise from and sink into the saddle at the trot.

PULLING: Removing hairs from the mane to make it neater and of even length.

Q

QUALIFIED: Hunter who has a certificate attesting that he has hunted satisfactorily for at least one season with a recognized or registered pack.

QUARTERING: An English term meaning to quickly groom so as to remove stable stains and tidy up a horse.

QUICK-RELEASE KNOT: A knot that is secure, but quick and easy to undo in an emergency.

R

REARING: When a horse rises up on its back legs.

REFUSAL: When a horse stops in front of a fence instead of jumping over it.

RIGHT HAND TO RIGHT HAND: When two riders pass each other with their right hands and the horses' right sides are facing.

RIBBONS OR ROSETTES: Ribbons are usually awarded to the top six places in most show events.

RUB RAG: A type of cloth that you use after grooming to remove dust from a horse's coat.

RUNNING UP THE STIRRUPS: Sliding the stirrup irons to the top of the leathers.

RUNNING OUT: Running out to the side in front of a fence instead of jumping over it.

S

SADDLE STAND: A wooden or metal frame to rest a saddle on for cleaning.

SADDLE PAD: A soft pad that is put under the saddle to absorb sweat and to protect the horse's back

SADDLE SORES: Sores that can form on a horse's back due to an ill-fitting saddle or dirty pads.

SCHOOLING: Teaching a horse to do something; practicing.

SEAT: How a rider sits on a horse or pony. If you have a "good seat," it means that you are secure on your mount.

SHAD BELLY: A formal dark swallowtail coat for showing or hunting.

SHYING: When a horse jumps sideways from something that frightens him.

SILKS: The jacket and cap worn by a jockey in racing. Each set of silks has a particular pattern and color combination that is used to identify the horse's owner.

SNAFFLE: A type of bit that has rings on both sides of the mouthpiece.

SOUND: A horse that is not lame.

SOUR: A horse that has had too much schooling, too much abuse, or too much jumping will become sour and oppose the rider's command.

STALLION: A male horse that is used for breeding.

STALL REST: When a horse is confined to his stall to recover from an illness.

STIRRUPS: A loop, ring, or similar device suspended from a saddle to support the rider's foot. Stirrup irons are made of metal, usually stainless steel.

STOCK UP: When a horse's legs or ankles, usually the hind ones, become swollen with lymph indicating a need for exercise or kidney trouble; if only one leg is "stocked up" it is usually from injury.

SULKY: A lightweight, two-wheeled cart used in harness racing.

SURCINGLE: A belt used to keep a blanket or saddle in place.

SUSPENSION: When all four legs are off the ground for an instant during the gallop.

SWEAT SCRAPER: A piece of equipment you use to remove excess water from the horse's coat after washing.

T

TACK: A general term for the saddle, bridle, girth, and other equipment used to ride a horse.

TACKING UP: Putting on the tack in preparation to ride.

THROATLATCH: The strap attached to the headstall, which fastens loosely under the horse's jaw.

THROWING A SHOE: When a horse loses a shoe by accident.

TRAIL RIDING: Riding out in the open countryside. Should never be done alone for safety reasons.

TRANSITION: Changing from one gait to another.

TREE: The frame inside the saddle.

TROT: One of the horse's natural gaits. It is faster than the walk but slower than the canter.

TROUGH: A large basin of water, usually in a paddock or pasture, which the horses can drink from.

TURN OUT: To put a stable horse out in a pasture or paddock for exercise.

U

UNSOUND: A lame horse.

V

VICE: A bad habit, such as cribbing, rearing, biting, bucking, or bolting that is potentially destructive to the horse or rider.

W

WALK: The slowest of the horse's natural gaits.

WEAVING: A nervous habit, usually a result of boredom, when a horse rocks from side to side in the stall.

WITHERS: The base of the horse's neck, where it joins the body above the shoulders.

WHIPPER-IN: A member of the hunt whose job it is to keep the pack together by calling or snapping a whip.

Y

YEARLING: A horse or pony that is one year old.

Z

ZEBRA: Horses, asses, and zebras belong to a single
family of mammals called the Equidae.

ZEBROID: The offspring of a zebra and a horse.

ZEDONK: The offspring of a zebra and a donkey.

SECTION FIVE
IT'S NOT JUST YOU

The evolution of the horse is not only very interesting, it is also paramount to the overall understanding of this incredible animal. Learning how a horse works from the inside out will increase your ability to ascertain his current state of wellness. Horses, not unlike humans, are targets for disease and injury. Quick and accurate assessment of their condition, along with proper medical attention, will return your horse to a solid state of wellness. A

Sailor

basic understanding of the more common illness can result in your being better able to tend to your mount. The day-to-day care of your horse and your things is an ongoing process and can never be left undone. Lack of attention to the needs of your horse can, in some cases, be fatal. He has worked very hard for you, and you should show your appreciation by giving him the best care available.

A HISTORY OF THE HORSE

Archeologists and paleontologists tell us that the horse preceded humankind by many ages, but little is known of its history earlier than 2000 B.C. What information we do have comes to us by studying the fossil skeletons found centuries deep in our earth. Interestingly, those horses judged to be the earliest were found in the Mississippi Valley area of the United States, but died out, for reasons unexplained, near the end of the last Ice Age.

The early skeletons show that the *Eohippus,* from which our present-day horses descended, was equal in size to a fox and not unlike him in conformation (the overall shape of a horse, and the way it is put together). The Eohippus was short-legged and had toes instead of hoofs. His development was quite slow. There is evidence that a larger species of the wild horse, the *Mesohippus,* was plentiful during the Stone Age and was used as a source of meat for the humans of that time. The Mesohippus was about

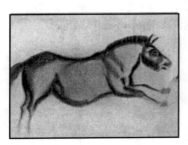

the size of a current-day sheep. Thousands of these skeletons have been found piled at the opening of a cave near Lyons, France.

During the Bronze Age, humans, having already

mastered the skills of herding sheep, cattle, and goats, began to herd horses as well. These herds were used for the purpose of supplying meat, but may also have been used as a source of milk. The nomads in Central Asia still use horses as a source of milk today.

The Mesohippus thrived in areas containing rich, plentiful vegetation resulting in their overall growth in size. In remote parts of western Mongolia a small scrubby horse can still be found today. So stunted in growth, this animal is only marginally larger than his toed ancestors. Intensive inbreeding and scarce sustenance are, no doubt, responsible for its lack of development.

Further proof of arrested development was found not long ago in the Grand Canyon of the United States. In 1940, a band of horses was discovered, on a high plateau, virtually isolated and all but inaccessible. How they got there will very likely remain a mystery, but it is obvious they have been residents of this location for a very long time. Again, inbreeding and a lack of plentiful food caused their stunted growth resulting in their being less than half the size of their mustang forebears.

The first visual proof we have of the horse existence, aside from fossils, is documented in the prehistoric cave paintings in France. The primitive drawings/paintings on the cave walls vividly depict the horse to be smaller and shaggier, but without question the forebear of the horse we know today. Considering their size, these early horses were probably first used to pull carts as opposed to carrying man.

Using the Parthenon frieze for example, we see the Greek horse to be very compact and round-bodied with little indication of wither (the base of the horse's neck, where it joins the body above the shoulders) or backbone. One can observe men riding on tolting (tolt is a fifth gate or way of going) horses of similar size as the present-day Icelandic Horse. The method of sitting is typical, and there are clear examples of tolt in the movement and position of the horses' feet. Considering the Greeks rode bareback, this would have been the most comfortable type of mount and would have been the direction taken in their selective breeding process.

When the horse became a servant of humans, it was probably no larger than a small pony. To keep all of this information in visual perspective, remember that in the year 3000 B.C., humankind was also considerably smaller than the people of today. This will help in producing a clearer mental picture. In remote areas of the world, where the horse has been left to shift for himself, he is still just as he was centuries ago. Quality care, proper nutrition, and, most important, selective breeding started the horse on his way to developing into the animals we know today. Breeders from centuries past obviously recognized these areas to be essential even so long ago.

Clearly, the history of man has been so dependent on the horse that it could not be written without them. The figure of humans on horseback remains a symbol of power and strength. The ancient Greeks had almost as great an admiration for the horse as they had for the human figure. One can see the loving care the sculptor lavished on both the human and the horse in his marble carvings. Until the domestication of the horse and humans learning to ride this magnificent animal, travel had been dependent upon one's two feet. With the realization that the horse was better suited as a means of transportation, rather than as a food source, the boundaries of exploration became endless, and thus the adventure began. The dependence on and the respect for the horse became paramount.

The horse was unknown in America when the Spanish conquistadors set foot on her shores. The Spaniards' conquest was made easier because, initially, the Indians were terrified at the sight of the horse. The Spanish horse, of Arabian and Barb blood, was noted for its toughness and endurance. From a handful of these horses, which either escaped or were later stolen by the Indians, the Western Plains became populated with large herds of wild horses. Captured and broken by the Indians and later by the white man, these horses became the broncos of the vast lands of the American west. These wild horses have survived for centuries on grazing land containing bone-enriching calcium. Horses do not need the lush, wet, low-lying pastureland required by such animals as dairy cattle. They can survive and flourish on their own in all types of weather and varying temperatures if given enough space to roam in search of new grazing land.

One particular horse that is a direct descendant of the horses brought to America by the Spanish conquistadors in the sixteenth century is the Appaloosa. The Nez Perce Indians developed this distinctively marked and very popular saddle horse. The name Appaloosa is derived from the Palouse Valley in Idaho, where this tribe of Native Americans lived. Not all horses with spots are Appaloosas; there are only six pattern types permissible in the breed with most of these horses having vertical stripes in their hooves. These compact horses make wonderful trail horses as well as competitive show horses and can now be found in many countries other than the United States.

In the early days, the Moors and Arabs did the most to improve the breeding of horses. No other breed has had a greater influence on horse breeding as a whole than the Arab. These horses were developed by the desert tribes of Arabia to suit their needs in battle, in transportation, and as a friend and companion.

The Crusaders of the twelfth and thirteenth centuries purchased many of these horses and transported them back to England. The Arabian horses were much too small to support a knight who, in full armor, weighed nearly four hundred pounds. They were, however, in great demand as pleasure-riding stock. The development of gunpowder rendered the need for armor and the lance useless, and this smaller breed of horse came into its own. Their bloodline was significant in building the foundation of the English Thoroughbred yet to come in the eighteenth century.

The Barb also played a part in the development of the Thoroughbred, although not to the extent of the Arab. Originally bred in Morocco and Algeria, the Barb was first taken to Spain by Muslim invaders during the eighth century. From there, they were transported to South America by way of the conquistadors and eventually found their way to England during the seventeeth century. Barb blood was mixed with that of the existing riding horse and played its part in the overall development of the English Thoroughbred.

The Andalusian breed owes its origins to the Barb as

well and can be seen displaying their elegant strides in many Spanish ceremonial processions. The Andalusian is usually a bay (brown body with black mane, tail, and lower legs) or a gray, and it averages around 15.2 hands in height.

It is nothing short of miraculous that from a single source could there be such a variety of individuals. Among wild animals there is almost always a general uniformity in their size and physical abilities. There is no such range in any other species as there is in the world of horses. Consider the size difference between a child's pony and the massive Percheron, and the variant speed differential between the small gallop of a Shetland pony and the blazing force of a Thoroughbred racehorse. Only through selective breeding for centuries could humans have achieved such results and what results they have been. Today, we enjoy a hugely diverse sport with an equally grand horse to fit each and every niche.

Horse anatomy

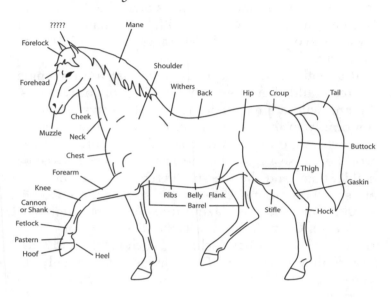

Horse skeleton

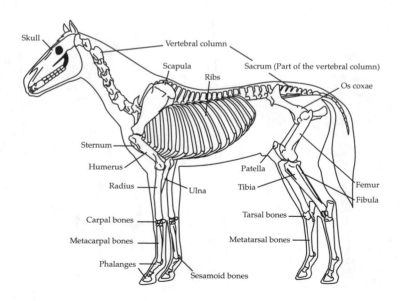

Horse muscles

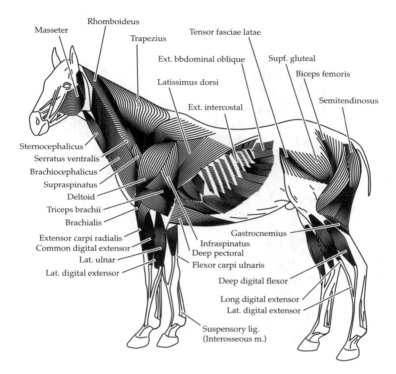

Horse skull

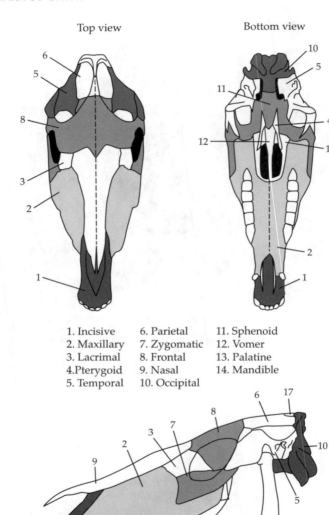

Top view

Bottom view

1. Incisive	6. Parietal	11. Sphenoid
2. Maxillary	7. Zygomatic	12. Vomer
3. Lacrimal	8. Frontal	13. Palatine
4.Pterygoid	9. Nasal	14. Mandible
5. Temporal	10. Occipital	

COMMON EQUINE ILLNESSES AND HOW TO IDENTIFY THEM

There are many injuries, ailments, and illnesses that can befall a horse at any given time. If your horse shows any peculiar behavior, has obvious signs of stress or discomfort, or displays any alarming abnormalities, this author strongly suggests that you call your veterinarian immediately. I would also suggest that you purchase an equine medical reference book. This type of text can be of great service when trying to understand and digest the terminology used in explaining what is wrong with your horse.

Below are listed just a few of the more common maladies you may hear discussed while at the barn. A working knowledge of these various conditions will give you a place to start on your road to understanding the overall necessity for providing your horse with the quality care he deserves.

DISTEMPER OR STRANGLES

Distemper or strangles is a common and contagious disease that affects horses, particularly while they are young, but can, however, affect older horses as well. Just like many human childhood diseases, once a horse recovers from a bout with strangles, he is usually immune for life. The name "strangles" refers to the narrowing of the upper airway as a result of the swollen lymph nodes in the head, jaw, and throat. Strangles is most likely to occur when a horse is being moved to new surroundings (transporting often causing stress) or where large numbers of horses are stabled, such as a breeding facility.

Symptoms

The first symptoms of strangles include a loss of appetite and general apathy, followed by a thick, white nasal discharge and a cough. Soon after these symptoms appear, the lymph nodes in the horse's head start to swell. The nodes usually affected are under the jaw; however, in some more serious cases, those all over the body can also swell. The swollen nodes are very painful and will eventually break open and allow the pus trapped inside to drain, thus relieving the pain.

If you suspect your horse has strangles, call your veterinarian right away so that treatment can begin. This treatment will consist of giving the horse medication, along with a recommendation that you keep him in a clean, quiet shelter, and out of drafts. It is also very important that the horse be kept isolated, as strangles is very contagious. Remember also to thoroughly clean and disinfect all tack and equipment used by the infected horse, including his stall.

EQUINE INFECTIOUS ANEMIA

E.I.A., as this disease is commonly referred to, is a very serious disease of the blood that usually results in the death of the horse. It is characterized by fever, the horse being lethargic, a general weakness, and loss of weight. E.I.A. is also known as swamp fever, a name it earned because it appears most commonly in the lowlands of the South and Southwest (from Virginia to Texas).

While this disease is contagious, it doesn't affect all horses, and some horses carry the germs without showing any symptoms. Fortunately, a test has been devised that can determine if a horse is a carrier. This test is called a Coggins Test (named for the veterinarian who first described it), and involves the veterinarian drawing a blood sample from the horse. The blood sample is then sent to a laboratory for examination. If the test results are negative the owner of the horse is issued a certificate stating the results.

States vary in their requirements for a Coggins Test, but most require proof, by way of certificate, that a horse has a "negative Coggins" before being allowed to travel between states. It is also a requirement of most sanctioned horse shows, that all horses competing are able to produce a current Coggins certificate.

This test must be performed on an annual basis. The only time a test is not required is when purchasing a horse as a foal; however, be sure to ask to see the dam's current Coggins certificate.

INFLUENZA

As with humans, influenza, or the "flu" as we call it, is rarely fatal among horses. It is most common among, but not confined to, young horses, and after it recovers the horse will usually have built up some immunity. Flu is contagious and is most commonly found in areas where groups of horses are kept together.

Symptoms

The symptoms of the flu occur about a week after the horse has been exposed. They include a fever, loss of appetite, a cough, and a watery nasal discharge. Horses showing any signs of having the flu must be put on stall rest immediately to prevent further complications. The horse should not return to work until all symptoms are gone, including the cough, which can last for quite some time.

There is a vaccine on the market that offers protection from some strains of influenza. It is not necessary for all horses to have this shot, but if he is in training, on the horse show circuit, or just before being transported between states, it would be wise to first have him inoculated.

LAMINITIS

Laminitis, better known as founder, is a common affliction that could usually have been prevented. The term laminitis simply refers to an inflammation of the laminae, which are located between the horny wall and the coffin bone in the hoof. When a horse founders, the laminae becomes swollen and inflamed. Because the hoof wall is solid, pressure builds causing extreme pain.

Laminitis or founder can be caused by any number of factors; most are preventable by simple quality horse care and attention to the animal's surroundings. For example: certain anti-inflammatory drugs, excessive intake of grain or lush pasture grass, drinking too much cold water when he is hot, and overwork on hard pavement resulting in road founder.

Symptoms

Signs of founder would include a rise in body temperature, a reluctance to move (take a step), heat in the feet, and an obvious reaction to pain when a hoof tester is used. Founder affects the front feet and a horse with founder will extend his neck and move his hind legs forward in an effort to relieve the pressure from his very sore front legs.

If you think your horse is suffering, and he is suffering, from founder, call your veterinarian immediately. The veterinarian can administer cortisone or antihistamines to reduce swelling, if he feels this is required. While you are waiting for the "vet" to arrive, don't give the horse anything to eat, remove his shoes if you can, run cold water over the affected area, or allow the horse to stand in cool mud.

NAVICULAR

Navicular disease, as its name implies, affects the navicular bone, which is located toward the back of the hoof (the heel). The deep flexor tendon glides over the bone and the disease can damage this tendon and the surrounding cartilage as well as causing disintegration of the bone itself. Navicular disease only occurs in the forelimbs and most often in Quarter Horses and Thoroughbreds, particularly geldings.

Symptoms

The symptoms of a horse with navicular include: he will often stand with one foreleg out in front of the other, he will display lameness, or a short choppy stride. Complete recovery from navicular rarely happens because you cannot take the weight of the horse off of his heels. The horse can have some corrective shoeing in an effort to relieve some of the pressure, but that is about all you can do.

THRUSH

Thrush is a degenerative condition of the frog (thickened, horny area in the middle of the sole) most easily recognized by the blackening of the affected area and by a pungent odor. Thrush usually occurs when a horse is forced to remain in unsanitary stall conditions, causing excessive moisture to the frog. It can also be a result of days in a muddy pasture, leaving the horse with packed hooves.

The prognosis for a horse recovering from thrush is good to excellent, provided that his housing receives a serious upgrade, all dead or infected tissue is removed, his feet are cleaned on a regular basis, and a topical antiseptic such as iodine is applied.

COLIC

Colic is a general term used to define a variety of stomach ailments that occur all too often in horses. The problem lies with the horse's stomach itself: it is quite small considering the overall size of the animal, a horse cannot regurgitate, and he has an inferior digestive system. The stomach of a horse is not equipped to handle even the minor problems of overeating or spoiled hay.

Symptoms

If the horse displays a swollen stomach, painful gas, lack of bowel sounds, or the inability to pass solid waste through the rectum, he very likely has colic. The horse may also paw at the ground, look at or bite at his sides, roll on the ground, and continues to lie down and get back up. If you think your horse is suffering from colic, call your veterinarian immediately. Take all food away from the horse and take his temperature.

There are several day-to-day things you can do to reduce the risk of colic: worm your horse frequently; feed your horse small amounts of grain twice a day; make sure all hay and grain are mold-free; water your horse at least twice a day (water aids in digestion); limit the time spent eating lush, green pasture grass; never feed grain to a hot and tired horse; and if you change the horse to a different kind of grain, do it gradually over the course of several days.

CRIBBING

Cribbing is more serious than wood chewing and is a very disagreeable habit. Cribbing occurs when a horse bites down on a hard surface and sucks in air. It is not particularly damaging to the hard surface, but is very bad for the horse. Horses that "crib" are more subject to colic and have trouble staying fit. They will also display this very undesirable behavior in and out of the stall.

STABLE CARE

Quality care for your horse includes proper maintenance of his surroundings. Try and think of your horse as a two-year old child in that he cannot do much for himself and will get into most everything if given the opportunity. Keeping the stall clean, properly laid, and dry is very important. Thrush is a degenerative condition of the frog area of the hoof and can be caused by unsanitary stall conditions. This should never happen if you clean your horse's stall at least twice a day, after his breakfast and again, following his supper. Your trainer may ask you to muck out your horse's stall. This means that you are to clean out both the solid and liquid waste.

After you have finished mucking the stall, you will need to replace the lost bedding and rake the stall. Be very careful to leave enough clean, dry bedding so the horse does not come in contact with the stable floor. Work to build up the bedding on the sides of the stall. This should remind you of snow drifts when properly done. These banks of bedding will help to prevent your horse from being stuck when he lies down. This state of being stuck is called "cast."

There are many different materials that can be used for bedding. The area in which you live can play a large part in what your barn uses. Two of the most common kinds of bedding are wood shavings and clean, dry straw. Both are very good materials, and whatever you use is mostly a matter of availability and personal preference.

The area around your barn needs to be cared for as well. All solid waste should be removed on a daily basis. Leaving piles of droppings on the ground will result in an overpopulation of insects, sour grass, and it is simply nasty.

When working around the barn, take the time to make sure all storage doors are closed, especially those leading to the grain and hay areas. Your horse can colic from overeating and that can be fatal in severe cases. Always close and latch gates and return the lids on any open containers. Take the time to pick up any trash, spent nails, and equipment, and put them in their proper place. Rinse off shovels and picks, and hose out the wheelbarrow before putting them away.

Here are a few of the basic necessities for insuring a clean barn.

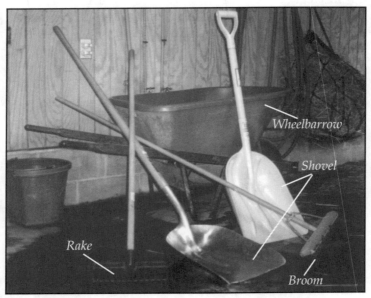

Photo by Jane Slaughter

GROOMING

A horse that lives in a stable should be groomed on a regular basis. It is best to groom your horse when his coat is dry. You will find it much easier to remove dirt and dander from a dry coat than if your horse is wet. If your horse lives in a pasture, he should not be groomed as often. Too much brushing of a pasture horse will remove the natural oils in his coat, which help to make him waterproof.

When brushing your horse, stand away from his body a bit so you can put your body weight into the motion of brushing. Try to always start at the top of his head, just behind his ears and work your way to the rump. A stiff bristle brush will do a great job removing dried mud and dander. Be very careful not to use a hard brush on your horse's head. Use a softer brush on his face so as not to bump or scrape the bony areas of his head.

Use extra care when brushing your horse's tail. It takes three years for horsehair to grow from the top of the horse's tail to the ground. Avoid using conditioners or sprays containing alcohol. This will cause the hair to become brittle and break off. Use your fingers to pick out foreign matter, knots, and run through any tangles.

Most horses enjoy being brushed and may even fall asleep during the grooming process. If your horse tries to nip at you while being brushed, it is not always a sign of aggression. Some horses are ticklish just like people and will react when you brush over their tickle spot. Your horse could also have a sore or burse lying under his coat, and when you stroke the brush over the injured area, it hurts. Brushes come in a wide variety and they each have their individual purpose. When starting to fill your brush box for the first time, select a few ranging from soft to hard. You can add to your original purchase if need be as time goes by.

You will also need to add a rubber or plastic curry comb to your brush box. Curry combs serve several different needs. They are used to remove shedding hair from your horse and should be used in conjunction with a stiff bristled brush. A curry comb will help improve your horse's circulation and is an excellent choice at bath time. The curry comb is also one of the best ways to clean your body brushes. Make sure to tap the curry comb and brushes against a hard surface to knock off any residual dust.

Hoof picks are very important, and you only need one of these. Shop around for the variety with the metal pick on one side and the very stiff brush on the other. Never ride your horse without picking his hooves. Run your hand down the back of his foreleg, and pick up the hoof. Always hold the front of the hoof in your hand. This gives the hoof the support it needs and also helps to protect you if your horse were to kick out. Gently pick out the hoof from the horse's heel to his toe. Turn the hoof pick over using the brush side, and sweep away any remaining dirt. Picking your horse's hooves removes mud, stones, and pieces of trapped material, which could otherwise cause lameness.

The next addition to your brush box is two good sponges that are different colors. They should be of the block variety and sized to fit your hand. Choose one of your selected colors and always use that one to wipe dirt from your horse's nose, eyes, and ears. Dampen the sponge before you begin; gently wipe around the

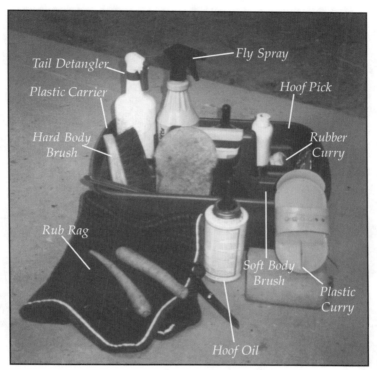

Photo by Jane Slaughter

eyes; remember to rinse the sponge out before moving on to the nose and ears. Rinse your sponge clean after each use. The other colored sponge is used to clean the dock area of your horse. Gently move the horse's tail out to one side and with the dampened sponge in the other hand, wipe the area under the tail. Wash your hands and the sponge after each use.

A rub rag will add a polished look to your horse by removing any lingering dust. Dampen the rub rag before using being careful not to get it too wet. Bunch the rag up in your hand and start wiping from behind the horse's ears moving in the direction of the hairs. This final polishing will leave his coat with a glossy sheen.

Hoof oil is necessary for a stabled horse. Bathing horses removes much of their natural body oil, and a loss of oil in the hoof can cause serious problems. Read the labels carefully to make sure it is an oil-type product and not one that contains alcohol or other drying ingredients. Paint each hoof starting at the forelegs remembering to always hold the leg while applying the oil.

The brush box itself should be of the plastic variety with a central handle. There should be a divided space in the middle on the underside of the carrier that allows the tote to balance on stall doors or fence railing. The wooden boxes are lovely to look at, but offer little in the way of practicality.

THE WASH STALL AND BATHING

Washing your horse is an important part of his overall grooming and good health. It is not always necessary to use shampoo, but you should at least rinse him off with the hose. NEVER put your horse away if he is dirty or wet with sweat. This can cause a variety of skin problems and may result in developing sores. Plus, it is simply not nice to the horse!

Most stables have an area known as the wash stall. Many times it is the only area of the barn that has a concrete floor, hot and cold running water, and a floor drain. Not only is this the place where you bathe your horse, it is also where you wash out his buckets, and apply necessary medications, wraps, and dressings.

Your barn might have shelving down one side to house supplies or you may carry your things, using a plastic tote, from your own storage area. Some of the things you will need to bathe your horse are easily purchased at your local tack shop. You will need a bucket, horse shampoo, mane and tail detangler, a sponge, a rag to wipe his face, and a sweat scrape to remove the excess water.

Using the water hose, wet your horse down from head to tail on one side. Don't use an excessive amount of shampoo. Remember, what you put on the horse must wash off of the horse. Scrub vigorously, but not so hard as to hurt the horse. Rinse that side THOROUGHLY before moving to the other side. Once you

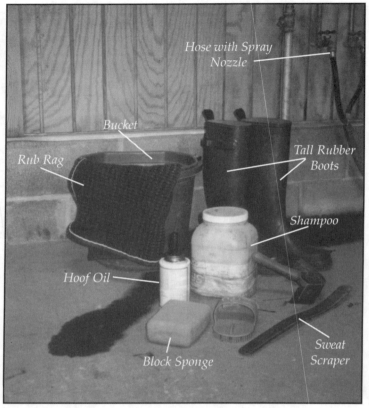

Hose with Spray Nozzle

Bucket

Rub Rag

Tall Rubber Boots

Shampoo

Hoof Oil

Block Sponge

Sweat Scraper

Photo by Jane Slaughter

have washed both sides of your horse, rinse over his whole body just to insure there is no shampoo left anywhere. Take the sweat scrape and start behind his ears and work going with the direction of his hair. The final step before leaving the wash stall is wiping his face with the clean rag.

If the weather is nice, take him outside to eat grass while he dries. If it is cold, make sure to use a blanket made for wicking up moisture so your horse does not catch a cold. Once the horse is dry, he should be brushed before he is returned to his stall.

YOUR TACK AND TACK ROOM

Leather tack is expensive and must be properly cared for and stored correctly. Abused or ignored tack can dry out, crack, and even become covered in mold. All of these situations are totally unacceptable and should never happen.

Your tack should be cleaned after each use. There are many products on the market made solely for the purpose of cleaning leather tack. Once you have finished cleaning your saddle and bridle, return them to their proper place. Most barns and stables have a designated area of the barn called the tack room. The tack room usually has a double row of wall-mounted saddle racks and a chorus line of bridle brackets. Each rider has a designated area, and it is usually labeled. Also, each horse has a bridle bracket with his name placed on the wall above. Never get the bridles confused because the bit on that bridle is just for that particular horse.

Most riders have a tack trunk or container of some sort to house their things. This container is usually kept on the floor underneath their saddle. It holds their helmet, chaps, extra saddle pads, towels, crops, and many other things. Organization is the key to keeping this area neat and keeping up with your "stuff."

Most stables have very strict and very necessary rules about cleanliness and order. You can rest assured that

Photo by Jane Slaughter

you will be reprimanded if you do not adhere to this set of rules. Quite often there are posted signs around the barn area reminding you of the obvious. Listed below are just a few of my favorites:

- No Whining!
- You used it, you clean it
- You broke it, you admit it
- Your horse dropped it, you shovel it up
- You got it dirty, you get it clean
- You unwrapped it, you roll it back up
- You took it out, you put it back
- Your mother does not work here
- Yes, you are precious, and yes, you will clean the **WHOLE** horse

SHOEING

Not only are the Celts of Gaul given credit for crafting the first curb bits, but they are also thought to be the inventors of the first nailed horseshoes as well. The Celts, known as the foremost ironworkers of the ancient world, were established in Britain by 450 B.C., and it is quite possible that they were shoeing horses prior to the Roman invasion.

Many people would question why horses need shoes. Some, usually dads upon receiving their first farrier bill, would add that wild horses do not wear shoes nor did the horses of earlier times. All of these people would be correct; however, working horses do need shoes. Horses who travel on hard ground need shoes, as do horses that live in wet conditions. Shoes can also correct some conformational defects, which were a result of birth defects, accidents, or disease. Horseshoes are not for adornment; they are for protection, ease of movement, and a way of improving the horse's natural ability to grip with his hoof. These "air equestrians" constructed from steel or aluminum help prevent damage to the hoof. An unshod horse working in adverse conditions would surely break, tear, or splinter the horn of his hoof, rendering the horse lame or sore-footed.

Fitting a horse with shoes also prevents the hoof from being worn away too quickly. On average the horn (the hard outside wall of the hoof) grows between ¼ and ¾

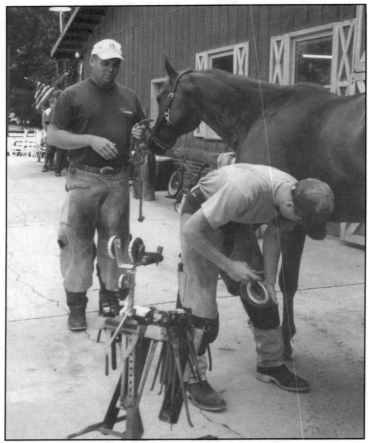

Pictured: Dean Newsome and Casey Spainhour

inches per month. With this in mind, a horse will need new shoes every four to six weeks. Allowing too much time between shoeing can cause damage to the horse's foot.

Fitting a horse with a new pair of shoes is an individual process. Each horse has his own needs and shape of hoof. Before the farrier can actually nail the shoe to the horse's foot, a great deal of preparation must be done. If your farrier does not do these things, please let him go and find a new one.

First the nail ends, or clenches, are cut off. This is the part of the nail, which protrudes to the outside of the hoof. After they are loosened, the shoe can be gently pulled away from the hoof starting at the toe and going backward toward the heel.

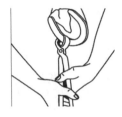

Next the farrier will clean and trim the underside of the hoof using a drawing knife. This very sharp instrument has a point curved backward allowing the farrier to stroke toward himself and safely scoop away unwanted hoof material.

Using a pair of hoof cutters, the farrier snips away the surplus growth from the past four to six weeks and then uses a rasp (a very coarse file) to level the hoof on the underside.

It is very important that the hooves are all the same length and level, so great care should be taken at this stage.

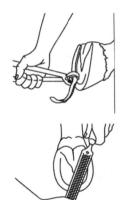

The next step basically has the same end result, but can be accomplished in several different ways. Horses can be hot-shoed or cold-shoed. One version of hot-shoeing is actually making a pair of horse shoes from a raw piece of iron. Farriers are required to do this to earn their Journeyman's certification. The other type of hot-shoeing is when the farrier uses heat and anvil to shape a pair of premade shoes. The heat from the red-hot shoe will make a brown line on the horse's hoof. This allows the farrier to make any ad-

 justments to the shoe resulting in a perfect fit. Horseshoes come in sets of two and can be reshaped by using the heavy hammer, an anvil, and no heat. This process is called cold-shoeing. Cold-shoeing is thought to be less desirable because the farrier cannot see exactly how the shoe fits.

One of the last steps is nailing the shoe to the horse's hoof. Using as few nails as possible, because an abundance of nails can weaken the hoof wall, a farrier will try for the ideal six nails, but no more than eight, if necessary. All nails should be in the out-  side of the hoof wall. Setting a nail in the wrong place can cause a horse to abscess. If you hear the word "quicked" that is what has happened. Think of your own fingernails and what happens if you injure the quick. OUCH!

 The final step is done on the outside of the hoof. The nail ends are pinched off and turned to form clenches. Using the rasp, the farrier will give the hoof a final going over and will also run under the clenches so they can be hammered down.

Running lightweight sandpaper over the entire hoof will result in a polished and finished look.

A quality shoeing job should closely resemble a fine pedicure. The hoof should appear even, clean, and bal-

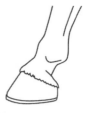

anced. There are many different styles of horseshoes and each has its purpose. The type of shoe used on your horse is very important and will need to be discussed with you, your trainer, and your farrier together if at all possible.

Your farrier will wear a pair of loose-fitting leather chaps or a divided, leather apron. This protective leg covering cushions his leg from the horse's hoof and shields his leg from the potentially dangerous tools. Shoeing a horse is very hard work and requires a great deal of bending and supporting of the horse's hoof. A farrier will always hold the hoof either between his knees or on top of his thigh depending on his needs.

All photos in this section by Jane Slaughter

From left to right: clinch cutter, hoof pick, shoe pull-off, nipper, hoof knife, driving hammer, and block.

*From left to right: rasp, nail puller, hoof gage (measures angles),
clincher, and rounding hammer.*

The piece of equipment below is called a shoeing box
and carries most of a farrier's most commonly used tools.
It is equipped with casters so as to move about as
needed.

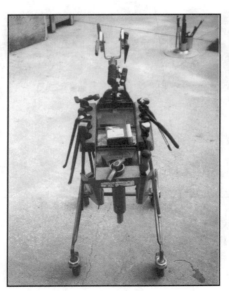

This piece of equipment is called a foot stand. The center post is used to support the horse's hoof and is used for the final stages of shoeing.

Below you will see a farrier's anvil stand. Most equipment used by farriers today is portable, but still very heavy.

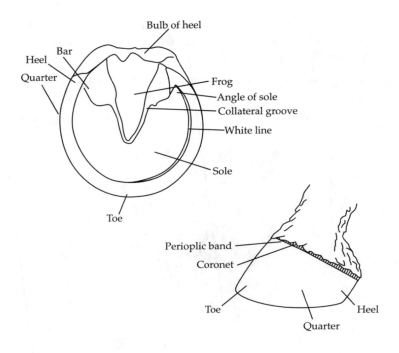

SECTION SIX
DISCIPLINES

In an effort to show how some things can be as different as night and day, and yet equally quite similar, I have chosen to highlight seven disciplines of English riding. The horse and the woman equestrian are the obvious common denominator. The individual sport, its history, and how women broke down the gender barrier, are the numerator that keeps life interesting. As you will read, it was never easy and success came with a price tag of injury, ingenuity, and sometimes, sheer guts. I am sure you will agree, that their courage deserves our applause as well as our appreciation.

DRESSAGE

The word Dressage comes from the French verb *dresser*, meaning, "to train" the horse. Dressage has evolved into a pleasure sport enjoyed by millions of people throughout the world, but got its beginning more than two thousand years ago. The object of dressage is to develop a true partnership between the rider and the horse, resulting in an almost dance-like display of athletic ability both longitudinally and laterally.

Prior to Greek antiquity, little is known about earlier civilizations and their techniques used in training horses. Bits and pieces of information have survived, in the form of clay tablets from Mesopotamia. Through this fragmented source of information, it would appear that they used a snaffle bit containing spikes, that were pushed into the horse's mouth. This brutal bit would indicate that the desired result was to control the horse using brute strength as opposed to sensitivity.

It was the Greeks who realized the horse's psyche to be an important factor in the horse's overall ability to perform. This realization took riding from the rough physical activity of the past and elevated it to the level of an art form. The Greek commander Xenophon (c. 430 to 345 B.C.) demonstrated in his detailed descriptions of classical equitation, that the Greek's response to the horse was two fold; in one of refinement as well as practicality.

"It is profitable to take the horse into battle, but if it carries itself elegantly and nobly then you must not tug at its mount and must take care not to hit it with the spur or the whip..."

Classical dressage disappeared into almost total obscurity when Rome fell at the hands of the barbarians in A.D. 410. During the Dark and Middle Ages, Europeans used a much heavier and thick-bodied horse. These animals needed to possess the ability to support the great weight of the armor-clad rider and the maneuverability of the horse was lost. Interestingly, it was the invention of gunpowder and, thus, firearms that returned the agile and hot-blooded horse to the forefront.

The Renaissance period originated in Italy, but quickly spread throughout Europe. With this "new birth" attitude among humans, dressage experienced a revival as well. Remembering that the small firearms had now replaced the lance, military leaders had to return to the drawing board to design a completely new battle plan. The military minds of the time also realized the need to replace the heavy horses used earlier with a much more agile and swift breed.

The terms used in today's dressage are of military origin. For example, the *piaffe* lent itself as a spring for sudden advances. The *levade* is a highly collected half-halt used for reaching down with a slash of the sword, to aim a pistol, or as a tactic of evasion. The *pirouette* could be used to wheel away from or toward the enemy. The *courbette*, which rockets the horse high into the air, would quickly disperse foot soldiers. The *capriole*, a giant leap into the air, was used as an effective means of escape taking the horse and rider over the heads of the infantry. It was of the utmost importance that a horse possessed the ability to perform *flying lead changes*, resulting in absolute mobility on the field of battle. Of course, today the *haute école* movements are

Photo from the collection of Max E. Ammon

Lis Hartel

taught solely for the purpose of exhibition.

In 1580, the Imperial Austrian Stud began importing Lippizanners from Spain. Keep in mind that the
Liberian horse was the only hot-blooded horse available in Europe. The wars with the Turks had prevented
the importing of Arabians, and the English Thoroughbred was not developed until much later in the 1800s.
It was from these horses that the Spanish Riding School
was created and finalized in 1735 by Charles VI. His
portrait still hangs in the school in honor of his contribution to the sport.

The Spanish conquistadors are given credit for bringing dressage to America. Their style of riding directly
influenced the western seat and stock saddle. Having
only the conquistadors as models, the Native Americans rode sitting upright at the walk and trot, but used
a forward seat at the gallop.

The first Olympic Dressage games were held in Stockholm, Sweden, in 1912. Only cavalry officers were allowed to participate in these equestrian games. The requirements of these early games included: collected and extended gaits; rein-back; turn on the hocks; four flying lead changes on a straight line; and jumping five small obstacles, one of which was a barrel in motion rolling toward the horse.

The United States Cavalry stationed at Fort Riley, Kansas, won Olympic team bronze in dressage in 1932. U. S. Captain Hiram Tuttle earned an individual bronze medal for the United States. It was also during this Olympics that the 20-by-60 meter arena with lettered markers was introduced.

Women first competed as Olympic equestrians in 1952 at the Helsinki Olympics. Lis Hartel was the lady who put women on the map in the arena of female Olympic equestrians. This was an incredible feat due to the fact that she had to retrain herself to ride after recovering from polio. Lis went on to earn the silver medal for Denmark in this event.

It is interesting to note that over the course of 2,500 years, the history of dressage has remained steadfast to its origin. The Greeks believed, and the dressage enthusiasts of today agree, its purpose is to maintain harmony between the rider and the horse, achieve lightness and balance, and above all, to be humane, keeping the horse happy and proud.

EVENTING

Like so much of our equestrian heritage, the history of eventing (also known as Combined Training) lies in the battlefields of yesteryear. Eventing was developed as a means of testing the endurance, speed, and obedience of the cavalry horse, as well as, the ability of the military rider. In French, eventing is *concours complet*, which translated means the complete test. In 1902, the French hosted the *ChampionatduCheval d'Armes* competition in Paris. This event consisted of a dressage test, a steeplechase, a 30-mile race over roads and tracks, and a jumping test.

The first Olympic three-day event was held in 1912 in Stockholm, Sweden, and participation was limited to military riders. Only active-duty Army officers, riding military horses, were allowed to compete for the United States. The competition was a test geared toward a military mount and the qualities needed for carrying out certain tactics. For example, elegance and obedience on the parade ground would parallel the skills needed for close combat; stamina, versatility, and courage were necessary attributes for a horse while engaged in battle; cross-country endurance was important for traveling great distances for the purpose of delivering important dispatches; and the horse's jumping ability in an arena proved his overall fitness and ability to actually leap over foot soldiers. It was also believed that the final test of show jumping was added to increase public interest in eventing.

Eventing involves three elements and is spread over equally as many days. In 1924, civilians were allowed to participate in Olympic Eventing competition. Non-commissioned Army officers, however, were not allowed to compete in the Olympic games until 1956, and women were banned from participation until 1964.

Perhaps one of the greatest factors in the encouragement of eventing as a sport was the establishment of the Badminton Horse Trials, in 1949, on the Duke of Beaufort's estate in Gloucestershire, England. The title "Badminton Horse Trials" was used instead of "Badminton Three-Day Event" to avoid confusion with the racquet game that originated in Badminton House. The actual dimensions of the official badminton court are still today an exact measurement of the room in which the game began. The 10th Duke of Beaufort offered his estate to be used on an annual basis for the Three-Day Event. Considering the vast amount of land needed for horse trials along with three days of horses, vehicles, and thousands of spectators trampling the manicured grounds, the Duke's generosity was nothing short of astounding. It was also an added plus that the Duke was an excellent horseman and a Master of the Hunt.

Horse trials are based on a step-by-step progressive approach to qualifying. There are five levels of recognized competition, beginning with novice (beginner level), which is a one-day horse trial only with fence heights of 2 feet, 11 inches. Training is the second level and is also limited to one-day horse trials consisting of 3-foot 3-inch fences. The last three steps are three-day events consisting of preliminary, which is one star and has fences measuring 3 feet, 6 inches; intermediate, which is two stars containing jumps of 3 feet, 9 inches; and advanced, which possesses three stars and obstacles measuring 4 feet in height. The Olympic level of three-day eventing is defined as four stars in difficulty, and all jumps measure 4 feet or higher.

A horse and rider must earn the right to compete at each level. As the horse and rider progress up the ladder in levels of competition, the bar of difficulty is raised accordingly. The overall winner in an eventing competition is determined by first converting the dressage scores into penalties, adding to that any penalties incurred from the other two parts; the person with the lowest amount of penalties is declared the winner. In eventing, there are competitions for both teams and individuals.

The dressage phase takes place on the first day of the three-day event. This test reflects its origin in the need for the cavalry officer to have an obedient and attractive horse on the parade ground, and the ability to make quick and decisive moves on the battlefield. The horse and rider are required to perform a set of movements that are committed to memory, while a panel of three judges awards points for the horse's pace, impulsion, and submission to the rider's directions, as well as for the rider's position on the horse and the use of aids. Any errors or incorrect sequences of required movements result in the subtraction of points.

Day two is the speed and endurance phase, which covers about 16 miles and is key to the competition. It is also the most exciting and challenging part of any eventing competition, attracting a large number of spectators. The speed and endurance part of the competition contains four parts. The first section contains a series of short roads and tracks that lead directly into the second phase, the steeplechase course (approximately 2 miles in length), which spills into phase three, a section of long roads and tracks. At the end of this phase there is a compulsory 10-minute break before continuing to the final phase. During the break, the horse will be checked by a veterinarian. The fourth and final phase is a grueling 4½-mile cross-country course containing thirty-two fences. Many of the jumps are actually combination jumps (containing more than one jump), which would increase the number of obstacles to more than thirty-two jumps. Each phase is separately timed and requires a variety of specific challenges. The cross-country section carries a time penalty, as well as points taken off for refusals, and run-outs, both of which are considered to be jumping faults. The whole process adds up to about 1½ hours of effort and the word "effort" is raised to a higher level in eventing.

Before the horse is allowed to participate in the final day of competition, he must pass a required series of veterinary inspections conducted after the speed and endurance section. In the stadium section of the test, a horse is judged on his ability to navigate a jumping course without penalties for knockdowns, refusals, falls, or exceeding the allotted time.

Completion of the three-day event by a horse would result in his having proven himself "fit for further service," to use the original military term. Surely no one having witnessed this incredible display of raw courage, stamina, and horsemanship would disagree.

After World War II, women began to demand that they be given the same consideration in the equestrian arena as was given to men. No longer would they stand passively by to their exclusion due to gender. Since the early 1950s women have pretty much done it all and done it successfully in serious competition on horseback.

With England being the origin of foxhunting, it is not surprising that the British are also the originators of the three-day event, often referred to as eventing, venue as well. Several British women made significant contributions to this sport proving early on that women were equal to the test of this rigorous sport. In 1954, Margaret Hough was the first woman to win Britain's premier event, called Badminton after the estate and course on which it is run. Sheila Willcox won the race three consecutive years beginning in 1957. Even British royalty has experienced success at the famous Badminton event with Princess Anne, daughter of Queen Elizabeth, taking fourth in 1974.

Taking her first jump at the tender age of three, Great Britain's Virginia Leng helped women find their place in the history books of three-day event competition. She has been perhaps one of the most successful women of this sport becoming a two-time Olympic medalist, five-time European champion, and a two-time world champion in the incredibly demanding three-day event.

Born in February 1955, Virginia was the daughter of an officer in the Royal Marines. She, as did most children of the military, grew up on the move, living all over the world. Regardless of her father's post, there was never a time when she did not ride horses. As a child, Virginia was a member of the Pony Club and gives credit to participating in the Juniors as her springboard to success as an adult.

Several serious injuries, to herself and her horses, over the years, nearly squashed her chances of continued competition. Virginia was considered to be a candidate for the British Olympic team in 1976 after winning a Canadian pre-Olympic three-day event in 1975. Unfortunately, Virginia took a serious fall in a later race breaking her arm in 23 places. Her doctors first considered amputation, but fortunately, opted to try and repair the arm instead. She was back at Badminton in 1977; this time, however, it was her horse Tio Pepe who suffered injury to his front legs, causing them to break down. It was at this point that Virginia Leng considered retirement. Little did she know that success was waiting for her at home in two different stalls in the barn.

Priceless and Night Cap were two horses Leng had purchased out of the same sire. The vet told her that

Photo by Kit Houghton

Virginia Leng

Priceless was unsuited to participate in the difficult three-day event. Fortunately, she ignored the veterinarian's critique of her new mount, and together they rode into the history books, winning the European Championships in 1981 and 1985, the Badminton title in 1985, and world championships in 1982 and 1986. Priceless earned his name by also helping Virginia win a team silver and individual bronze medal in the 1984 Olympics in Los Angeles.

Night Cap won his share of three-day events and honors as well. Virginia Lang was once quoted as saying, "Neither Priceless nor Night Cap ever had any trouble whatsoever. And I'm sure it was because they were never pushed, particularly at one-day events, and they were never run in bad ground. And they were never run if they had the slightest small problem like a sore knee or a stifle that wasn't quite right."

Horseback riding, especially competitive riding, has always been primarily an endeavor of privileged society. Virginia Leng's middle-class upbringing, however, is a case in point of what can be accomplished if desire and commitment are stronger than one's pocketbook. Faced with the reality of being unable to personally support her riding and competition, Virginia began knocking on the doors of corporate London in an effort to secure sponsorship. Finally, after much searching, she was able to convince the British National Bank to underwrite her expenses. Later she was quoted as saying, "In the end the only reason I succeeded was because the (bank) chairman's wife was fond of horses!"

FOXHUNTING

Humankind has hunted, whether for food or pleasure, since the beginning of time. The Cro-Magnon man created brilliant drawings on cave walls in southwestern France roughly 17,000 years ago at the beginning of the Magdalenian Age, showing theirs to be a life of hunters and gatherers. From that time forward, humans began to adapt to a more agricultural way of life, with the eventual rise of cities and towns. Hunting then became more supplemental to their diet rather than their total intake of nourishment.

The sport of organized foxhunting began in Great Britain and can be traced as far back as the Norman Conquest (1066). The traditional quarry of the first hunts was the stag and the bear, later adding the hare. Not until the end of the seventeenth century did the English begin to hunt the fox.

In most cases the foxhunts of two hundred years ago were all-day affairs and slow-going ones at that. The hounds were bred for their tongue and scenting abilities rather than for speed. Add to the mix that there was very little to no jumping and you had quite a dull day compared to the standards of today's hunts.

Originally, hunting was a sport enjoyed exclusively by the wealthy landowners in Britain and Ireland. However, over the years, as much of their land was sold and developed into farmland, more and more people from all walks of life were invited into this close-knit circle.

With this inclusion of ministers, butchers, tailors, doctors, and lawyers, hunting became more organized and competitive as well. It also became of great benefit to thousands of people. The employment rate of the time increased significantly as the demand for clothing, saddlery, hay and grains, blacksmiths, horse breeding, and farm workers rose to an all-time high. Hunting quickly became a large part of England's economy as opposed to a sport of the idle rich of days gone by.

Foxhunting was brought to North America by the early colonists and was enjoyed by a variety of individuals. The earliest known record of hounds being brought to this country was on June 30, 1650, when Robert Brooke settled in Maryland along with his family and hounds. Colonists began to establish foxhunting as a sport in Maryland, Pennsylvania, and Virginia by the early 1700s. The earliest existing record of an organized hunt for the benefit of a group of hunters, rather than for a single land and hounds owner, was in Virginia in 1747 by Thomas, sixth Lord Fairfax. Much of

Image courtesy of the National Sporting Library

George Washington

that original tract of land is still used for hunting by the Blue Ridge Hunt Club today. American foxhunting has always centered on the chase as opposed to the kill.

George Washington, the first president of the United States, was an avid foxhunter, owned his own pack of hounds, and was a Master of the Hunt. Much of what is known today about the quarry, organized hunts, and the land used is found intertwined in the diaries of President Washington. Many of his entries tell about foxhunts near the nation's capital. One particular entry clearly outlines a day while congress was in session and the hounds ran close by the capital in "full cry." Apparently, many of the congressmen bolted outside to watch and simply could not resist the temptation to participate. Jumping on their horses, they quickly followed and joined the chase. Inside the capitol, one could probably hear the pounding of the gavel declaring a recess.

The organization of American hunting is much the same as that of Britain and Ireland. Most hunts are subscription or membership packs. This type of organization is similar to many golf or tennis clubs, in that one pays a membership fee to be on the hunt roster. Annual membership dues are used to feed and care for the hounds as well as for any hunt association expenses. The typical season of foxhunting is from the time the crops are harvested in the midfall until they are once again planted in the spring. The winter months were traditionally when the land lay dormant. Foxhunting requires large areas of land to be successful and, with rural development, holding on to such premium property is becoming more difficult.

Members of the hunt elect a Master or Joint-Masters and they serve for a designated period of time. It is the Master's responsibility to organize the day, lead the hunt, oversee that proper care is being given to the hounds, and maintain a good relationship with the owners of the land on which they hunt. If the hunt master does not lead the field himself, he will appoint a field master. It is the job of the field master to keep the field of riders close enough to enjoy watching the hounds without getting in the way of the master. Whippers-in assist the huntsmen in hunting the hounds. They also work to prevent the hounds from running onto roads or land not designated for hunting. There will also be a person responsible for closing gates and someone else to supervise the juniors and hilltoppers (those who follow at a slower pace or even by car). A hunt will also have a secretary whose job it is to take care of administrative requirements such as making sure that all horses participating have current Coggins tests. A horse with a positive Coggins test or no test documentation at all is not allowed to hunt.

Louise "Loulie" Eustis was the daughter of George Eustis Jr., a member of Congress from Louisiana. Loulie's grandfather on her mother's side was William Wilson Corcoran, a merchant banker who invested in a curious, some called it silly, invention of Samuel Morse's called the telegraph. Her grandfather Corcoran also owned an extensive art collection in Washington, D.C., that became the cornerstone of the gallery that still bears his name. Celestine "Tante" Eustis, her unmarried aunt, adopted Loulie after the death of both of her parents when she was just a little girl. Aunt "Tante" decided that it would be better for the frail six-year-old to live in a more moderate climate, so in 1873 Loulie, her two brothers, and Aunt Tante moved to Aiken, South Carolina. The once frail young girl grew to become a healthy and avid horsewoman.

In 1890, Loulie married Thomas Hitchcock. The Hitchcocks were considered to be one of America's foremost sporting families in the early part of the 1900s. Thomas Hitchcock was well known for his abilities as a horseman, but it was Mrs. Hitchcock who developed Aiken, South Carolina, into a prominent equestrian cen-

Photo by Freudy

"Loulie" Hitchcock

ter. Thomas Hitchcock, William C. Whitney, and Thomas' brother Frank, purchased an 8,000-acre tract of land in Aiken, naming it Hitchcock Woods. It was in the Hitchcock Woods that Thomas and his wife Loulie hunted their private pack of hounds. They also invested in farmland along with Edwin Morgan in the area around Westbury, Long Island. Thomas and Loulie named their estate Broad Hollow. Some of their neighbors included the Belmonts, Whitneys, Winthrops, and

Morgans, all sporting families themselves. Theodore Roosevelt, a family friend and fellow foxhunter, lived just down the road in Oyster Bay.

Louise "Loulie" Hitchcock is considered to be one of the "first ladies" of fox hunting. She was also one of the first women to actually sit astride when riding as opposed to hunting sidesaddle. She, along with her husband Thomas Hitchcock, are considered to be cornerstones in turning Aiken, South Carolina, into the horse country it is today.

Julian L. Peabody, eldest grandson of Mrs. Hitchcock, wrote of his grandmother, "She really loved it all. I think she never was happier than when she was mounted on a good horse and was riding over jumps in the hunting field or in the Aiken drags." In his book *Gran*, Mr. Peabody recounts several occasions when his grandmother, Loulie, rode with her arm in a sling, her leg in a cast, but her spirit was never daunted or discouraged.

Louise Eustis Hitchcock was a very important woman in the equestrian world. On the day after Christmas in 1933, Mrs. Hitchcock took a nasty fall while leading a drag hunt for children in Aiken. She suffered several fractured vertebrae in her neck and passed away on Easter Sunday the following year at the age of 67. She lived life to the fullest and her love for horses enriched the world in which she lived.

Currently there are 171 organized clubs in North America, and the popularity of foxhunting continues to grow. In a world quickly being engulfed by steel and asphalt, the thrill of galloping across an open field behind a pack of hounds in full cry has no measure. Rarely will you find a more outspoken group of individuals in their desire to protect the quarry and preserve the environment. Today's hunters deeply appreciate the privilege to participate in an age-old sport and treasure the memories for a lifetime.

POLO

The sport of polo was born over 2,600 years ago and has lost none of its reputation as "the game of kings." Persian rulers originated the sport of polo in 500 B.C. History records this society to be the first to sit astride their horses and hit a small ball across a field with a wooden mallet. The name Polo comes from the Tibetan word "pulu," which is the same word used for the root from which the original ball was made.

In later years, the British colonials came to know the sport of polo while in India and brought the sport back to England in the nineteenth century. Still later, the game was introduced in Argentina, which now produces some of the world's best players. History credits James Gordon Bennett for having introduced the sport of polo to American society in 1876. Australia, England, and South Africa are recognized as leading polo-playing nations of this now global sport. Polo is played on all five continents and in about 50 countries, but it is still the aristocratic sportsmen who give superb performances on horseback. It is also symbolic of a sophisticated lifestyle that is reflected by the spectators as well. Polo tournaments have maintained a reputation for being key social events with the "stomping of the divots" between chukkers, for example, as well as, high-class sporting competitions.

Teams, containing four players each, participate on

a field measuring 274 by 182 meters. The objective of polo is to hit the ball with precise blows through the opposite team's goal. After each goal, the direction of play is reversed. The team that puts the ball between the goal posts (7.5 meters apart) most often during the course of up to 10 chukkers (a period of time not unlike a quarter in basketball), each lasting 7½ minutes, is declared the winner.

Great importance is attached to fair play and the well-being of the swift, agile polo ponies. The "polo pony" is not actually a pony, but rather a small horse measuring over 14.2 hands. (As there were no modern devices of measurement, such as today's rulers or yardsticks, one's hands [turned sideways] were used to account for height.) Some of the best polo ponies come from South America, especially from the country of Argentina. It is very important that the mount be extremely flexible, have amazing powers of acceleration, and be able to make quick and sudden changes of direction as required by the sport. The best polo ponies also tend to exhibit above-average equine intelligence. These horses also need to possess great courage to withstand the aggressive play of the game. The term "riding off" is the way in which one player can gain possession of the ball from another.

Striking the leather ball accurately at breakneck speed requires long hours of practice. A polo player must first begin to learn the game from the back of a wooden horse. From there, the rider progresses to a stick and ball on the back of a real horse. Polo players are not unlike other competitors of equestrian sports and must maintain a diligent work ethic throughout their career if they choose to be successful. Tactical play is vital in the game of polo and an outstanding individual player is important. But, overall, polo is a team sport and each individual must exhibit true sportsmanship when on the field of play.

Eleanora Randolph Sears erased the notion of polo being a sport reserved only for men by becoming one of the first women polo players in the United States. She also played the game riding astride instead of sidesaddle, as was the custom for women at that time.

The great-great granddaughter of Thomas Jefferson, Eleanora Randolph Sears was born in Boston, Massachusetts, on September 28, 1881. As a child of privilege, Eleanora participated in a variety of sports enjoyed primarily by the socially elite. She was an excellent athlete, participating in tennis, squash, figure skating, and marathon walking, and is considered by most to be America's first true "sportswoman." Riding and equestrian sports, however, were her first and enduring love. Not only did Eleanora participate in the game of polo, she also maintained a stable full of racehorses and managed to ride nearly every day.

Eleanora Randolph Sears was not simply an accomplished equestrian. She was also an im-

Photo by AP/Wide World Photos

Eleanora Sears

mensely generous woman, offering her financial support, as well as some of her horses, to the United States Equestrian Team. The Boston Police Department was able to continue their mounted division as a result of Eleanora's donating some of her horses to their stable. Additionally, The National Horse Show was able to continue as an annual event due to her sponsorship.

Perhaps her greatest donation, especially to women, was her refusal to accept the social restrictions attached to females in regard to their behavior and in their dress. Eleanora passed away in 1968, but during her lifetime she paved the way for so many women to follow. She truly was a pioneer in every definition of the word.

RACING

The competitive racing of horses is one of humankind's most ancient sports. In fact, racing's origin can be traced back as far as the nomadic tribesmen of Central Asia, who were the first to domesticate the horse around 4500 B.C. Since the beginning of recorded history, horse racing has been and continues to be an organized sport in all major civilizations from Central Asia to the Mediterranean. For instance, chariot races and mounted horse racing were both recognized events in the Greek Olympics by the year 638 B.C. These sports grew in popularity to near public obsession in the day of the Roman Empire.

During the twelfth century, when English knights returned home from the Crusades, they brought with them swift Arab horses. This period of time is now credited as the origin of modern racing. Over the course of the next 400 years, more and more Arab stallions were purchased and bred to English mares producing the Thoroughbred, a horse with combined speed and endurance. Pairing the fastest of these fine animals, two-horse races involving private wager became a popular diversion of England's nobility.

During the reign of Queen Anne (1702-1714), horse racing in England became a professional sport and match racing gave way to races involving several horses on which the spectators participated in betting. With this newfound sport, race courses sprang up all over England. They offered increasingly large monetary rewards (purses) to the winners in an attempt to attract the very best horses. With the attraction of such money to be made, the focus on selective breeding and owning horses for profit became an industry in and of itself. With such rapid expansion of racing as a sport came the need for a central governing body. In 1750, England's racing elite met at Newmarket to form an official authority on the sport. It was named the Jockey Club and still presently exercises complete control over the regulations of English racing.

The newly formed organization wrote complete rules of racing and sanctioned race courses to conduct meetings under those rules. They also took steps to regulate the breeding of racehorses. James Weatherby, whose family members worked as accountants to the members of the club, was assigned the task of tracing the pedigree of every racing horse in England. And for generations, members of the Weatherby family have carefully recorded the pedigree of every foal born to the original racehorses of 1793. By the early 1800s, the only horses permitted to be referred to as "Thoroughbreds," were those horses listed in the *General Stud Book*. They were also the only horses allowed to participate in sanctioned horse races (recognized horse races, as opposed to, "backyard" wagers).

The British settlers brought the sport of racing horses to the colonies and laid out the first racetrack on Long Island, New York, as early as 1665. Although the sport of horse racing grew in local popularity, the development of organized racing in America did not begin until after the Civil War. But by 1890, there were as many as 314 tracks operating across the United States. The rapid growth of the sport, along with the lack of any central governing authority, led to the presence and eventual dominance of criminal elements. In 1894, however, in reaction to this, the nation's most prominent track and stable owners met (not unlike their English ancestors) to form the American Jockey Club. Ruling with an iron hand, this organization was successful in eliminating much of the corruption.

As a result, in 1908, the number of racetracks had fallen to a mere 25. This was mostly due to the anti-gambling sentiment that led most tracks to ban book-making. Ironically, it was in that same year that pari-mutuel betting was introduced at the Kentucky Derby. Pari-mutuel betting allows for a fixed percentage, 14 percent to 25 percent, of the total amount wagered to be taken out for track expenses, purses, and state and local taxes. This signaled a turnaround for the sport of horse racing. At the end of World War I, spectators flocked to the racetrack to watch such greats as Man o'War and racing prospered until the Second World War. There was a serious decline in the popularity of racing during the 1950's and 1960's, but that all came to an end in the 1970's with the running of Secretariat, Seattle Slew, and Affirmed. Winning the Triple Crown (the Kentucky Derby-first run in 1875, the Preakness Stakes-first run in 1873, and the Belmont Stakes-first run in 1867) took on a whole new meaning with the victories of these three horses and has become the top prize of today's racing sportsmen.

Julie Krone, was born on July 24, 1963; in Benton Harbor, Michigan, and became the winningest female jockey, with over 3,000 victories to her credit.

The daughter of Don and Judi Krone, Julie was raised on a ten-acre farm near Eau Claire, Michigan. She got her love for horses and riding from her mother, an accomplished equestrian in her own right. When Julie was two years old, her mother put her on the back of a horse, which then proceeded to trot away. Julie picked up the reins, gave them a tug, and turned the horse back in the direction of her mother. There was never any ques-

Photo by AP/Wide World Photos

Julie Krone

tion as to the direction her life would take and that riding was her love and given talent.

Julie racked up numerous ribbons and awards as a very young girl, but none quite as noteworthy as winning the 21-and-under division at the Berrien County Youth Fair horse show. That victory was quite an accomplishment considering she was only five years old at the time.

Regardless of the competition, Julie Krone always considered racing to be her first love. In the year 2000, she was named to the Thoroughbred Racing's Hall of Fame. To date, she is the only woman to have achieved this honor.

The attire of the jockey and the horse is also noteworthy. When racing, the jockey wears a set of silks, consisting of a jacket and cap in a particular pattern and color combination. The horse wears a matching saddle silk that is placed on his back under the saddle. Each racehorse owner or stable has a specific pattern and color combination for his or her silks, so that the horse and its owner can be easily identified. In a flat race (one without jumps), horses can reach speeds up to 40 miles per hour.

In the early days of racing, when a jockey had been caught doing something unacceptable, he was summoned to the office of that particular track or Jockey Club office. Considering most areas of any racetrack and the stable areas are composed of dirt, sand, shavings, and other materials, the office was the only elaborately decorated area of the complex. The phrase "called on the carpet" got its origin by a jockey being reprimanded in front of the official behind the desk while standing on the only carpet on the premises.

Finally, it is also very interesting to learn that, for example, at the Kentucky Derby, many of the horses' stalls are bedded with special hay grown only in Mexico. It is said to be the only hay in the world that makes no dust. The care given to these marvelous creatures called horses is, indeed, well deserved.

SHOW JUMPING

Show jumping is a relatively new sport that can be traced back to Dublin, Ireland, approximately 140 years ago. Prior to that time, jumping hurdles was limited to the sport of foxhunting, and the first recorded jumping competitions were actually developed as a test for hunters. Hosted by the Royal Dublin Society in 1866, show jumping began with a high and wide "leaping" competition on Leinster Lawn. One year later, in 1866, the Paris Show included a jumping class, but it was a cross-country test as opposed to being held in a stadium.

The 1900 Paris Olympic games included a variety of jumping competitions. These early competitions were divided into three groups: a timed "prize jumping" with top honors going to Haegeman of Belgium; a long jump test won by van Langendonk, a fellow countryman of Haegeman: and a high jump won by Gardieres, of the host country France, clearing a height of 6 feet, 13/16 inches. Equestrian sports were made a permanent addition to Olympic competition in 1906. Show jumping quickly became a sport enjoyed by spectators from all walks of life. The speed, agility, and aerial displays of strength exhibited by the horses along with the talents of the gifted riders brought record crowds to the competitions.

The sport of show jumping was given an additional boost by the creation of the International Horse Show at Olympia, London in 1907. This competition pulled out all of the stops creating quite a show and became the cornerstone of show jumping, especially during the years between the two World Wars. The International Horse Show was also the site for the first National Cup competition.

The development of standard international rules took some time to develop. Prior to World War II, each country had its own definition of knockdowns, jumps were constructed differently at various venues, there was no set time requirement to complete the course, and judging varied greatly between countries. It was very difficult for riders to compete internationally with all of this diversity in rules and equipment.

Following the Second World War things began to change for the betterment of the horse, the rider, and the spectator. A set of international rules was drawn and agreed upon, time became a factor that added excitement for the spectator, and with clarity being given to the rules, the onlooker became much more involved in the sport.

Carol Hagerman Durand is thought by many to be the "First Lady" of show jumping. She was the first woman to qualify for the Olympic team at Fort Riley, Kansas in 1951. Before the Olympics in 1952, however, the Olympic Committee decided to exclude women from participating in show jumping competition. The committee reversed its decision four years later, allowing women to compete for the first time in the area of show jumping.

Born in Kansas City, Missouri, Carol Hagerman was riding at the age of eight, and by her 20s was a rider in great demand by many leading Midwest exhibitors and horse dealers. She was also showing her own horses that she had trained herself.

During the war years, show jumping and most equestrian events were put on hold for obvious reasons. With

Carol Hagerman Durand

her riding career at a temporary standstill, Carol Hagerman joined the Red Cross and served for two years in India and China.

After the war, Carol, now Carol Hagerman Durand, was back in the saddle and in the winner's circle of competition. In 1950, she headed for Indiantown Gap, Pennsylvania, to compete for a spot on the first "civilian" United States Equestrian Team. Carol was successful in her bid for a place on the team and she, along with Norma Mathews and Arthur McCashin, began to tackle the fall circuit. This threesome, beginners if you will on the international circuit, proved their ability to compete globally with five victories in their first year and seven wins in the following year.

Carol was heartbroken by the decision of the Olympic Committee to exclude women from competition in 1952, but went on to compete internationally with the team at the world renowned Royal International Horse Show. That fall, the United States Equestrian Team posted its best showing to date by laying claim to twelve victories.

In 1970, at the age of 52, Carol Durand died tragically while trying a horse at the Cahokia Downs racetrack in Illinois. Survived by her husband, her son, and fans around the world, Carol Durand's extraordinary talent will never be forgotten. Mrs. Durand was inducted into the Show Jumping Hall of Fame in 2000.

Photo courtesy of The Chronicle of the Horse magazine, call 1-800-877-5467 to subscribe.

"Touch of Class"

Another famous female, this one being of the four-legged variety, was also inducted into the Show Jumping Hall of Fame in the year 2000. Touch of Class, a 16-hand bay Thoroughbred mare was the first horse ever to post a double clear round in Olympic history.

With Joe Fargis in the irons, she cleared 90 out of 91 jumps and brought home two gold medals, one individual and one team, from the 1984 Olympic Games in Los Angeles. The ability of this wonderful horse to put together one amazing round after another brought with it the admiration of the equestrian world and helped in her being the first nonhuman to win the United States Olympic Committee's Female Equestrian Athlete of the Year Award.

STEEPLECHASING

The roots of steeplechasing can be traced back to Ireland in the year 1752. This maiden race involved two Irishmen and, you guessed it, a church steeple. It would seem that two horsemen, a one Dennis O'Callaghan, and another gentleman named Edmund Blake, challenged one another to a match race (a race consisting of only two participants). The original race covered about 4½ miles from Buttevant Church to St. Leger Church in Doneraile in County Cork. With churches being the most prominent landmarks on the countryside at that time, and considering the height of their steeples, they provided the obvious start-to-finish markers. Due to the immense height of a church steeple, it was the only thing the human eye could see protruding into the sky from a great distance. The sport of steeplechasing began that day and took its name from the simple requirement of the contest, "chase from steeple to the steeple." History records that Mr. Blake won the race, therefore quieting the dispute, if only momentary, as to which man owned the fastest horse.

From this initial race, cross-country match races spread to England, with the first reported race involving more than two horses occurring in 1790 in Leisestershire, England, and has never lost its popularity in Britain. The most famous steeplechasing event in the world is England's Grand National and has been held in Aintee, England, every year since 1839.

In the United States, there are many well-known steeplechases. The U.S. Grand National Steeplechase is held annually at Belmont Park (a track race). Celebrating its 100th anniversary in 1994, the Maryland Hunt Cup races over tall post-and-rain fences. The National Hunt Cup in Radnor, Pennsylvania, dates as far back as 1909. November brings the much-loved Colonial Cup International held annually in South Carolina.

Steeplechasing possesses all of the thrills and speed of horse racing on the flat; add jumping to the mix, and one has an event not unlike human hurdle events exhibited in track and field. The rider is faced with two elements requiring intense focus: breakneck speed and concern for clearing the jumps.

A race containing National Fences offers the competitor man-made jumps consisting of steel frames, which are then stuffed with plastic brush, and foam rubber jump rolls covered with green canvas. These National Fences have been standardized since 1974 and are used at many of the major meets. Tractor-trailer trucks are used to ferry a set (enough for an entire meet) of jumps from meet to meet. Most hurdle races are 2¼ miles long, containing ten or more jumps, each measuring 4 feet, 4 inches in height.

Timber courses are permanent fixtures across the countryside consisting of approximately twenty fences with an average height of 4 feet and a course measuring between three to four miles in distance. The Maryland Hunt Cup is one of the most challenging timber races in the world, consisting of a four-mile course and vertical hurdles, some of which measure nearly 5 feet. The longer distance races measure the endurance of a horse as opposed to his speed.

The National Steeplechase Association, now in its 105th year, governs all jump racing in the U.S. setting rules, licensing participants, and granting sanctions to race meets. This association is headquartered in Fair Hill, Maryland, and the roster includes approximately 1,200 members. It is interesting to note that at present, there are only eleven states in America that participate in steeplechasing. These states fall mostly in the Southeast, Mid-Atlantic, and Midwest regions and collectively host approximately 32 races.

Attendance on race day offers a wide variety of spectators. On any given day there are novice equestrians standing alongside riders of national recognition, and college students listening intently to senior citizens as they recount race days from years gone by. The onlookers are able to be as physically close to the excitement as they choose. The view from aside a hurdle is exhilarating as spectators watch as the horses clear the brush, while feeling earth shake beneath their feet from the pounding of the horses' hooves.

Tailgating is also a traditional part of the day's festivities. The ambiance, as well as the bill of fare, enjoyed at these occasions is quite impressive including such things as; silver flatwear, candelabras, linen tablecloths, and culinary delights matching those served in many a fashionable restaurant. It truly is a wonderful day at the races, enjoyed by an estimated one million people annually.

In 1968, the world of male-dominated steeplechasing was turned up-

Photo by Douglas Lee

Kathy Kusner over the 13th fence

side down by a very determined Kathy Kusner. A two-time Olympic show-jumping rider, took the Maryland Racing Commission to court for a very long legal battle to acquire a jockey's license. Kathy insisted that the racing commission could no longer legally or ethically refuse to issue a license due to a rider's gender. The Maryland District Court agreed and ruled in her favor.

Unfortunately, Kathy was unable to compete in steeplechasing for several years due to a broken leg and her previous commitments to the United States Equestrian Team. In 1971, however, she became the first woman to ride in the Maryland Hunt Cup, finishing in sixth place out of a field of twelve. It is agreed by many that Kathy Kusner finished in first place in her efforts to break down the gender barriers in the sport of steeple-chasing.

AFTERWORD

I feel really flattered to have been asked to contribute to this book. Jane has done a wonderful job researching all aspects of women and riding. Her book addresses questions we have all wondered about but didn't know where to find the answers. I commend Jane for all her efforts in bringing this book and all its knowledge to us women riders.

I am not sure why I was asked to write except I have always had a passion for horses. I am very fortunate to have a mother who loved horses and also managed a barn and a riding program. We can all relate to this job; however, my mother raised seven children while doing so!

Horses have been a part of my life for as long as I can remember. I cannot imagine what my life would have been like without them. From the time I was in my first horse show at the age of four until now at age 50 plus, horses have always been there. Horses can teach you so much. They will humble you one minute and have you on a "high" the next.

I now have a barn and lesson program myself. I try to convey my love for these wonderful animals by teaching a lot of adult amateurs as well as children. Nothing is more pleasing or more rewarding to me than to hear, "I had fun today; thanks for the lesson."

When you ride only once a week it is hard to have a

relationship with your horse. I encourage all my riders to spend as much time with their horses as possible, grooming, grazing, or just hanging out with them. Each horse has a personality all its own, and I feel if you want to ride better or enjoy riding more, know your horse.

I have found over the many years of working with women riders that there are certain

Photo from the collection of Suzanne Lacy

women who are "horsewomen." They have a feel and connection with horses that cannot be taught. I can teach the mechanics of proper riding, but I can never teach them the "feel." These are the women who come to the barn just to be there.

Horses have a way of making you forget your problems for the moment. We have a rule at my barn—"Check your 'baggage' at the gate." Don't come to the barn with your troubles. Leave them, ride, and enjoy your time on and off your horse. When you have finished riding, things will be clearer and not really as bad as they seemed. On your trip home from the barn you can go back to reality. I think it is really important for women riders to take the time for themselves and their horses and just RIDE!

I have two grown sons and neither of them rides. When they were younger, I tried to get them to ride but they would have nothing to do with it. They had seen me come home too many times with too many bruises, etc. I explained to them that I could not imagine if they

Photo by Susan Brinkman

were to ask a young lady if she would like to go horse-back riding, the answer would not be YES.

I hope you have enjoyed reading this book as much as I have. I have learned so much and I hope you, the readers, or should I say "horsewomen," have learned as well. Jane has brought to us a real source of horse knowledge and a wealth of valuable information to be shared with horsewomen everywhere.

Suzanne Lacy

REFERENCES AND RESOURCES

REFERENCE: INTERNET ARTICLES

Almanac-People
The Learning Network Inc.
  http://lycoskids.infoplease.com/ipka/A0886842.html

Badminton Horse Trials History
http://www.horsenews.com/eventsum/badminton/
    history.html

Sisi-Elisabeth-Empress of Austria
http://www.geocities.com

Female Explorers
http://wwwlfemexplorers.com/article1006-2.html

Horse Daily
http://www.horsedaily.com/olympics/event3.html

Lady Godiva (Godgifu, in the spelling of her time.) by
Jerome C. Krause
http://www.abacom.com

Marie Antoinette Queen of France
http://www.2.lucidacafe.com

Marie Antoinette
http://www.newadvent.org

Mr. Horse: Polo-Origin and playing rules
http://www.mrhorse.com/sport/polo/originen.htm

MFHA-About Foxhunting
http://www.mfha.com

National Cowgirl Museum and Hall of Fame
http://www.cowgirl.net/cowgirl.aspx

Steeple Chasing-Sandhills Area Chamber of Commerce
http://www.sandhills.net/steeplechasing.html

The Evolution of Women on Horseback
Margaret Bennett, Canadian Horse Annual (1999)

The First Ladies' High-Heeled Shoe Author Unknown
http://www.aristotle.net

History of Dressage-Leslie A. Neumann-Horse Previews
Magazine website
http://horse-previews.com

The History of Dressage-Carolynne Stronczek for Beginning Dreamweaver
http://www.caspixel.com/dw6.html

The History of Horse Racing
http://www.mrmike.com/explor/hrhist.htm

The Horse in Human History-Melinda Maidens
http://ussers.erols.com/mmaidens/

The History of the Icelandic Horse
http://www.sunycgcc.edu

Horse History: An In-depth Chronology of North American Horses, Nancy R. Deuel, PhD
http://www.cavalry.org/Horse-History.html

Sandra Day O'Connor, U.S. Supreme Court
http://www.lucidcafe.com/library/96mar/oconnor.html

The Show Jumping Hall of Fame
http://www.showjumpinghalloffame.net

USET Disciplines
http://www.uset,com

Women of Achievement and Herstory Compiled and Written by Irene Stuber who is solely responsible for its content.
www.undelete.org/woa/woa09-28.html

REFERENCE: BOOKS

Anderson, C.W. (1963). *C. W. Anderson's Complete Book of Horses and Horsemanship*. New York: The Macmillan Company.

Bird, Isabella (1982). *A Lady's Life in the Rocky Mountains*. London: Virago.

Blyth, Henry (1970). *Skittles: The Last Victorian Courtesan The Life and Times of Catherine Walters*. London: Rupert Hart-Davis Ltd.

Clarke, Mrs. J. Stirling (1857). *The Habit & The Horse; A Treatise on Female Equitation*. Published by Authoress, J. Rogers, at Raby's, 46, Wigmore Street, Cavandish Square, "W"

Clayton, Michael (1992). *The Love of Horses*. New York: SMITHMARK Publishers, Inc.

Delort, Robert (1972). *Life in the Middle Ages*. New York: Greenwich House, Inc.

deRuffieu, Francois Lemaire (1986). *The Handbook of RIDING ESSENTIALS*. New York: Harper & Row, Publishers, Inc.

Edwards, Elwyn Hartley (1991). *The Ultimate Horse Book*. New York: Dorling Lindersley, Inc.

EYEWITNESS VISUAL DICTIONARIES (1994). *The Visual Dictionary of the Horse*. New York: Dorling Kindersley, Publishing, Inc.

Green, Lucinda (1993). *THE YOUNG RIDER*. London: Dorling Kindersley, Inc.

Hazard, Willis P. (1854). *Lady's Equestrian Manual*. Philadelphia: Kite & Walton.

Johnson, Anne Janette (1996). *GREAT WOMEN IN SPORTS*. Detroit: Visible Ink Press.

Karr, Elizabeth (1884). *The American Horsewoman*. Boston: Houghton, Mifflin & Co., The Riverside Press, Cambridge.

Kerswell, James (1991). *HORSES*. New York: Random House Company.

Mackay-Smith, Alexander, Druesedow, Jean R. & Ryder, Thomas (1984). *Man and the Horse, An Illustrated History of Equestrian Apparel*. New York: Simon & Schuster.

Mills, Bruce and Carne, Barbara (1988). *Horse Care and Management*. New York: Howell Book House, Inc.

Moore, Elaine T. (1953). *Winning Your Spurs*. Boston: Little, Brown and Company

Morris, George H. (1971). *HUNTER SEAT EQUITATION THIRD EDITION*. NEW YORK: DOUBLEDAY a division of Bantam Doubleday Dell Publishing Group, Inc.

Newark, Tim (1989). *WOMEN WARLORDS, An Illustrated Military History of Female Warriors*, London: Blandford.

Peabody, Julian L. (1999). *GRAN*. Howell Printing: Aiken, South Carolina.

Pickeral, Tamsin (1999). *THE ENCYCLOPEDIA OF HORSES & PONIES*. China: Barnes & Noble, Inc.

Podhajsky, Alois (1976). *THE ART OF DRESSAGE Basic Principles of Riding and Judging*. Garden City: Doubleday and Company, Inc.

Prideaux, Tom (1973). *Cro-Magnon Man*. New York: Time,Inc.

Siegal, Mordecai (1996). *UCDAVIS School of Veterinary Medicine, Book of Horses, A Complete Medical Reference Guide for Horses and Foals*. New York: Harper Collins Publishers, Inc.

Spencer, Herbert & Mayer, Fred (1971). *CHAKKAR POLO AROUND THE WORLD*. Zurich: City-Druck AG.

Watkins, David (2003). *BLACK BEAUTY-THE HORSE THAT WAS NEVER FORGOTTEN*. Middleburg: The Chronicle of the Horse, January 17, 2003.

Watson, J. N. P. (1986). *The World of POLO Past & Present*. Topsfield: Salem House Publishers.

Winants, Peter (2000). *STEEPLECHASING, A Complete History of the Sport in North America*. Lanham & New York: The Derrydale Press.

Woolum, Janet (1992). *OUTSTANDING WOMEN ATHLETES Who They Are and How They Influenced Sports in America*. Phoenix: The Oryx Press.

World Book, Inc. (2000). *The World Book Encyclopedia, Volume "G"*. World Book, Inc. Chicago, IL.

About the Author

I was born on April 7, 1951, in the small town of Ramseur, North Carolina, and enjoyed a wonderful childhood. My sixteenth birthday will always be considered as one of my best. That was the year I was given my first horse. Growing up in a rural area came with many perks, but it also meant that there were no  barns that gave English riding lessons. I taught myself to ride by working in the fields and up and down the back roads. A few of my friends also had horses, and we often rode together, as well as alone. Still, I dreamed of taking lessons and participating in horse shows.

From high school, I went on to college, earned a bachelor's degree in art education, got married, began teaching, and started a family. Over the next twenty years, my riding experiences were reduced to the occasional trail ride and that of being a horse-show mom.

Throughout all of this, however, I never lost sight of my personal dream. At the age of 46, I announced to my family that I had made arrangements to have riding lessons. I assured them that they would survive not always having me around and that they would actually be the better for it. At the age of 48, I attended my first horse show and even earned a blue ribbon.

I have loved horses for a lifetime. They are my passion and my peace. Little can compare to the smell, touch, and companionship of these magnificent animals. The tranquility of riding across a spring meadow, quietly grooming your mount, or just hanging out at the barn cannot by bought or bottled.